ESTÉRELLE PAYANY

BETTER MADE AT HOME

ORIGINAL   100% NATURAL   FRESH

PHOTOS | Guillaume Czerw

BLACK DOG
& LEVENTHAL
PUBLISHERS
NEW YORK

For Philippe, Virgile, and Rodrigue, the most helpful and dedicated testers.

For Oliver, Pierre, Nicolas, Delphine, Michel, Mireille, Caroline, Jérôme, Adrien, Gaétan, Mayalen, Patrick, Sophie, Valérie, Quitterie, Fanny, Cécile, and Julien, who meticulously measured, tasted, commented, and encouraged.

Originally published in France under the title
La Petite Épicerie du Fait-Maison

Published by
Black Dog & Leventhal Publishers, Inc.
151 West 19th Street
New York, NY 10011

Distributed by
Workman Publishing Company
225 Varick Street
New York, NY 10014

Manufactured in China

Cover and interior design by Sophie Dupuis-Gaulier

Photographs by Guillaume Czerw

ISBN-13: 973-1-57912-976-7

h g f e d c b a

Library of Congress Cataloging-in-Publication Data available upon request

CONTENTS

INTRODUCTION

The recipes of *Better Made at Home* enable you to create traditionally store-bought indulgences and many French favorites in your own kitchen Making them yourself takes a little time and creates something of a mess, but it's a heck of a lot more fun than buying them off the shelf. And while we're at it, we'll show you how to make staples such as ketchup and mustard (watch out, the mustard is hot!) and a chocolate-hazelnut spread that is scarily good. With this book you can even make your own leavener in seconds. But watch out: once you've tried these snacks, you'll find it hard to do without.

ON YOUR MARKS, GET SET, AND FILL YOUR
AT-HOME SHOPPING CART WITH YOUR VERY OWN "BRANDS,"
USING THE LABELS PROVIDED HERE.

CHOCOLATE-HAZELNUT **SPREAD**

MAKES:
ONE 8-OUNCE JAR

PREPARATION
about 10 minutes

COOKING
about 20 minutes

INGREDIENTS

4 ounces (100 grams) whole unsalted hazelnuts in their skins

4 ounces (100 grams) milk chocolate with hazelnuts, broken into pieces

⅓ cup (9 cl) unsweetened condensed milk

1 teaspoon unsweetened cocoa powder

1 teaspoon sunflower or nut oil

½ teaspoon pure vanilla extract

Pinch of salt

Imagine a rich chocolate spread flavored with hazelnuts. Sure, it's almost a sinful explosion of calories, but once tasted, it's impossible to resist.

| Heat the oven to 350°F (180°C).

| Spread the hazelnuts in a single layer in a shallow metal pan and roast for about 15 minutes. Remove the pan from the oven and let the nuts cool for about 5 minutes.

| When cool enough to handle, rub the hazelnuts between your fingertips to remove the skins. (You could also rub them with the folds of a clean dish towel to remove the skins.) Transfer the nuts to a food processor or blender and pulse for 2 to 3 minutes or until reduced to a fine powder.

| In a saucepan, heat the chocolate and condensed milk over medium heat until the chocolate melts. Stir occasionally to blend.

| Pour the hot milk mixture over the ground nuts and add the cocoa powder, oil, vanilla, and salt. Pulse several times or until the paste is smooth and evenly colored. Spoon the paste into a sterilized 8-ounce jar, seal and refrigerate. (For more on sterilizing jars, see page 140). The Butterella will keep for up to 2 weeks.

NOTE

YOU CAN USE SOUR CREAM THINNED WITH A LITTLE MILK IN PLACE OF THE CONDENSED MILK.

GRANDMA'S **STRAWBERRY JAM**

**MAKES:
THREE 8-OUNCE
JARS**

PREPARATION
about 15 minutes

REFRIGERATION
overnight

COOKING
about 15 minutes

INGREDIENTS

1½ pounds (600 grams)
ripe, top-quality
strawberries

1¾ cups (400 grams)
sugar

Juice of ¼ lemon

Homemade jam is surprisingly easy to make—and very sticky. We like how it "sticks" to bread and butter. To give the jam a touch of class and a slight sharpness, add three turns of the peppermill just before you remove the pan after boiling. No one will guess!

| Discard any bruised, unripe or overripe berries (if you discard more than 1 in 10, replace them with good berries). Rinse the usable berries, remove the stems, and chop the strawberries into small pieces.

| Transfer the berries to a mixing bowl, and add the sugar and lemon juice with 4 teaspoons (5cl) of water. Stir well, cover and refrigerate for 8 hours or overnight.

| Empty the bowl into a large saucepan and bring to a boil over medium-high heat. As soon as the mixture boils, use a slotted spoon to remove the strawberry pieces and set them aside.

| Cook the syrup remaining in the pan until it registers 220°F (104°C) on a candy thermometer. Return the berries to the pan and bring to a boil. Cook at a boil for about 10 minutes or until thickened.

| Fill sterilized, 8-ounce jars with the jam. (For more on sterilizing jars, see page 140.) Seal the jars with canning lids and rings and then turn the jars upside down to cool.

| The jam will keep at cool room temperature for 6 months. Once opened, it will keep for about 3 weeks in the refrigerator.

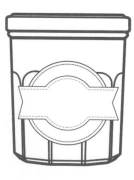

HAPPY **MUESLI**

**MAKES:
ABOUT 6½ CUPS
(650 GRAMS)**

PREPARATION
about 5 minutes

COOKING
5 minutes

INGREDIENTS

1⅓ cups (300 grams)
organic rolled oats

2 ounces (50 grams)
whole hazelnuts

2 ounces (50 grams)
dried apple pieces

2 cups (75 grams)
wheat flake cereal

2 cups (75 grams)
natural corn flakes

3 ounces (75 grams)
raisins

2 tablespoons
powdered milk

¼ cup (40 grams)
packed light brown
sugar

3 pinches of salt

What better way to start the day than with this tempting muesli sprinkled with milk or mixed with some natural yogurt. You could also mix it with fresh fruit.

| Spread the rolled oats in a large skillet and cook over medium-high heat just until they darken to golden brown. Slide them onto a plate to cool.

| Put the hazelnuts in the same skillet and cook over medium-high heat for 2 to 3 minutes or until lightly roasted. Transfer to a cutting board and coarsely chop them and the apple pieces.

| In a mixing bowl, toss the rolled oats with the chopped nuts and apple. Add the cereals, raisins, powdered milk and brown sugar. Season with salt and toss again.

| Transfer the muesli to an airtight container. It will keep at room temperature for about 3 months.

NOTE

THIS RECIPE IS FOR CLASSIC AMERICAN MUESLI, BUT IT CAN BE VARIED BY USING UNSALTED ALMONDS OR CASHEWS. YOU COULD ALSO ADD PUMPKIN SEEDS, BUCKWHEAT OR QUINOA FLAKES— THE POSSIBILITIES ARE ENDLESS.

CHOCOLATE COCONUT **CRUNCH**

Making baked muesli is a piece of cake and can be seriously addictive. Once you get started, try all sorts of add-ins. Here we add chocolate (your favorite kind) and coconut for an irresistible crunch. Prefer it without the hazelnuts? Want to add dried cherries? You decide.

MAKES:
ABOUT 2¼ CUPS
(600 GRAMS)

PREPARATION
about 10 minutes

COOKING
45 to 50 minutes

INGREDIENTS
2 tablespoons sunflower oil

1 cup (100 grams) packed light brown sugar

3 tablespoons honey

1 leaspoon ground cinnamon

3 cups (300 grams) organic rolled oats

2½ cups (100 grams) natural corn flakes

3 ounces (75 grams) chopped hazelnuts

¼ cup (50 grams) grated coconut

1 teaspoon salt

4 ounces (100 grams) bittersweet, semisweet, milk, or white chocolate, chopped into small pieces

| Preheat the oven to 300°F (150°C).

| In a frying pan, heat the oil over medium heat. Add the brown sugar, honey, and cinnamon and cook, stirring until the sugar dissolves. Remove from the heat.

| In a large bowl, mix the rolled oats with the corn flakes, hazelnuts, coconut and salt. Pour the melted sugar mixture into the bowl and stir to mix.

| Spread the mixture on 2 baking sheets and bake for 40 to 45 minutes, stirring every 10 minutes or so to prevent burning. Remove the baking sheets from the oven and let the crunch cool to room temperature.

| Return the cooled mixture to the bowl and toss with the chocolate pieces. Transfer the crunch to an airtight container. It will keep at room temperature for about 3 months.

CHOC-CHIP **BUNS**

These yummy breakfast buns are ultra moist and contain no milk or butter—but are deliciously studded with chocolate chips.

**MAKES:
30 BUNS**

PREPARATION
about 30 minutes

STANDING TIME
1 hour 15 minutes

COOKING
about 20 minutes

INGREDIENTS
2 tablespoons honey, preferably acacia or mixed flower honey

1 packet active dry yeast (each packet weighs ¼ ounce; 7 grams)

4 cups (500 grams) pastry or all-purpose flour (plus a little for kneading)

2 tablespoons raw, granulated sugar

¼ teaspoon salt

2 large eggs, preferably free-range

7 tablespoons (10 cl) sunflower oil (plus a little for the baking sheets)

2 teaspoons pure vanilla extract

¾ cup (160 grams) semisweet or milk chocolate chips

A little milk or 1 large egg, beaten, for glaze

| Put the honey in 1 cup (25 cl) of lukewarm water. Add the yeast and stir gently so that the yeast and honey dissolve.

| In a large mixing bowl, mix together the flour, sugar, and salt. Make a well in the center of the flour and break the eggs into it. Add the oil, vanilla, and then the yeast mixture and using a wooden spoon, stir until the liquid is absorbed by the flour.

| Turn the dough out onto a lightly floured surface and knead for about 10 minutes or until the dough is no longer sticky. Alternatively, this can be done in a bread machine or standing mixer with a dough hook. Return the dough to the bowl and cover with a damp dishtowel. Let the dough rise in a warm, draft-free place for about an hour or until doubled in size.

| Punch the dough with your fist to remove the air. Using your hands, spread the dough out on a work surface that is dusted with flour.

| Sprinkle the dough with the chocolate chips and knead it again to make sure they're evenly distributed.

| Divide the dough into 30 balls, each weighing 1 to 1½ ounces (about 40 grams). Put them on lightly oiled baking sheets and cover again with damp dishtowels. Let the rolls rise for about 15 minutes longer.

| Preheat the oven to 300°F (150°C).

| Brush the rolls with milk or beaten egg to glaze them. Bake for about 20 minutes or until they are round and golden brown. Let the rolls cool on wire racks.

| Serve right away or wrap in aluminum foil for up to 3 days. The rolls can be frozen, too, for a month or so.

SANDWICH **BREAD**

This bread is so soft it's pillowy, but whether you toast it or spread it with butter and jam, it will make you want to get up in the morning.

MAKES:
2 MEDIUM-SIZED
LOAVES

PREPARATION
about 15 minutes

STANDING TIME
about 1 hour 45 minutes

COOKING
about 35 minutes

INGREDIENTS
½ cup plus
2 tablespoons (15 cl)
skim milk

1 packet active dry
yeast (each packet
weighs ¼ ounce;
7 grams)

4 cups (500 grams)
all-purpose flour

2 tablespoons
granulated sugar

1 teaspoon fine salt

4 tablespoons (6 cl)
sunflower or canola oil
(plus a little to grease
the molds)

¼ teaspoon distilled
white vinegar

| Mix milk with an equal amount of lukewarm water (1¼ cups [30 cl] of liquid in all). Add the yeast and stir gently so that the yeast dissolves.

| In a large mixing bowl, mix together the flour, sugar, and salt. Make a well in the center of the flour and add the yeast mixture. Add the oil and vinegar and using a wooden spoon, stir until the liquid is absorbed by the flour.

| Turn the dough out onto a lightly floured surface and knead for about 10 minutes or until the dough is smooth and pliable and no longer sticky. Alternatively, this can be done in a bread machine or standing mixer with a dough hook. Return the dough to the bowl and cover with a damp dishtowel. Let the dough rise in a warm, draft-free place for about 1 hour or until doubled in size.

| Punch the dough with your fist to remove the air. Divide the dough into 6 pieces, each weighing about 5 ounces (150 grams). Roll these pieces of dough into balls on a surface that has been dusted with flour.

| Divide the balls between 2 lightly oiled loaf pans. Cover each pan with a damp dishtowel and let the dough rise in a warm, draft-free place for about 45 minutes. During this time the balls will combine into loaves.

| Preheat the oven to 350°F (180°C).

| Bake the risen loaves for about 35 minutes or until the bread is golden brown. Remove the loaf pans from the oven and then invert the bread onto wire racks to cool.

| Serve when cool. The bread will keep for 3 days stored in a paper bag on a lower shelf of the refrigerator. The bread freezes well.

NOTE

IF YOU DECIDE TO FREEZE THE BREAD, LET IT COOL COMPLETELY AND THEN SLICE IT TO PREVENT CRUMBLING. WRAP IT WELL AND PUT IT IN A FREEZER-SAFE PLASTIC BAG.

CHOCOLATE MILK POWDER

**MAKES:
ABOUT 15 CUPS
(550 GRAMS)**

PREPARATION
about 5 minutes

COOKING
1 or 2 minutes

INGREDIENTS
11 ounces (300 grams) milk chocolate, coarsely chopped

7 ounces (200 grams) bittersweet or semisweet chocolate

¼ cup (50 grams) unsweetened cocoa powder

2 tablespoons cornstarch

2 tablespoons granulated sugar

1 pinch of salt

This homemade chocolate powder might be a little less "instant" than you're used to, but it tastes so much better, so you'll be happy. Heat it with hot milk until thick and creamy and you will be in chocolate heaven!

| Using a food processor or blender, mix together the chocolates, cocoa powder, cornstarch, sugar, and salt.

| Transfer the mixture to an airtight container or jars with tight-fitting lids. The chocolate powder will keep for up to 6 months.

TO MAKE HOT CHOCOLATE, MIX ABOUT 14 TABLESPOONS (20 CL) (ALMOST 1 CUP) OF MILK WITH A HEAPING TEASPOON OF THE CHOCOLATE POWDER AND HEAT OVER MEDIUM-HOT HEAT. SIMMER RAPIDLY UNTIL THE HOT CHOCOLATE IS GOOD AND THICK.

MIXING MILK CHOCOLATE AND DARK CHOCOLATE MAKES THE COCOA POWDER GOOD AND SWEET WITH A HINT OF VANILLA. IF YOU PREFER YOUR HOT CHOCOLATE REALLY STRONG, USE DARK (BITTERSWEET OR SEMISWEET) CHOCOLATE ONLY AND ADD 2 MORE TABLESPOONS OF SUGAR AND THE SEEDS FROM HALF A VANILLA BEAN.

SWEDISH **CRISP BREADS**

There is far more to Swedish cuisine than smorgasbord. Try these little breads, sort of a cross between rolls and toast. The egg-shaped crisps are baked twice so that they keep longer than most.

MAKES:
28 CRISP BREADS

PREPARATION
about 25 minutes

RESTING
2 hours plus overnight

COOKING
30 to 35 minutes

INGREDIENTS

1 active dry yeast (each packet weighs ¼ ounce; 7 grams)

2 cups (250 grams) all-purpose flour

2 cups (250 grams) organic whole wheat flour

2 tablespoons granulated sugar

¾ teaspoon fine salt

1 tablespoon canola oil (plus a little for greasing the baking sheet)

| Dissolve the yeast in 1 cup (25 cl) lukewarm water. Stir to mix.

| In a large bowl, mix the flours with the sugar and salt. Make a well in the center and add the yeast mixture and the oil. Gradually stir the liquids into the flours with a wooden spoon until all the liquid has been absorbed.

| Turn the dough out onto a lightly floured surface and knead for about 10 minutes, or use a bread machine or a standing mixer with a dough hook attachment. Cover with plastic wrap or a damp dishtowel and let rise in a warm, draft-free place.

| Preheat the oven to 400°F (200°C).

| Coat your hands with flour and pick up the risen dough, letting the air expel as you do. Divide the dough into 14 equal pieces and mold them into little footballs about 3 inches long and 1 inch wide.

| Put them on a lightly oiled baking sheet, leaving plenty of space between them. Cover them with a damp dishtowel and leave for a further 30 minutes to rise again.

| Bake for about 15 minutes. Watch them closely so they do not overbake. They will not be completely baked at this point. Let the crisp breads cool for about 30 minutes on wire racks.

| Reduce the oven temperature to 350°F (180°C).

| Carefully cut the footballs in half lengthwise, using a fork to help, and put them back on the baking sheet with the cut sides up. Bake for a further 15 to 20 minutes or until golden brown.

| Turn off the oven and wedge the door open with a wooden spatula, leaving the crisp breads inside to cool overnight so that they're completely dry.

| Store the crisps in a tightly lidded airtight tin for up to 3 weeks.

DAIRY-FRESH **YOGURT**
USING A YOGURT MAKER

Using a yogurt maker is the simplest and quickest way to make yogurt. You don't even need to heat the milk. Make sure the yogurt maker is somewhere where it won't be jostled or moved (you don't want it on top of the washing machine, for example!).

| In a bowl or mixing jug with a pour spout, mix together the milk and yogurt with a wooden spoon or rubber spatula.

| Depending on the fat content of the milk and how thick you want the yogurt, add powdered milk and stir well. The more you add, the thicker the yogurt. If you use skim milk, use all 4 tablespoons of powdered milk.

| Put the yogurt maker on a stable, out-of-the-way surface. Pour the mixture into the pots in the yogurt maker, close the lid and switch it on, following the manufacturer's instructions. Leave the lid in place for 6 to 9 hours.

| Open the yogurt maker, put the lids on the pots and refrigerate them for at least 3 hours before eating. The yogurt keeps for 8 to 10 days in the refrigerator.

MAKES:
EIGHT 4-OUNCE (125 GRAM) POTS

PREPARATION
5 minutes

COOKING
6 to 9 hours

REFRIGERATION
3 hours

INGREDIENTS

3⅓ cups (80 cl) whole, low-fat or skim milk

½ cup (125 grams) plain, natural yogurt, store-bought or that you've made previously

1 to 4 tablespoons powdered milk (optional)

NOTE

THE FLAVOR OF THE YOGURT WILL DEPEND ON THE TYPE OF NATURAL YOGURT YOU USE. CHOOSE THE ONES YOU LIKE BEST AT THE STORE AND EXPERIMENT.

HOMEMADE **YOGURT**

MAKES:
EIGHT 4-OUNCE
(125 GRAM) POTS

PREPARATION
5 minutes

COOKING
3 hours in the oven;
8 hours in the pressure
cooker

REFRIGERATION
3 hours

INGREDIENTS

3⅓ cups (80 cl) whole,
low fat or skim milk

½ cup (125 grams)
plain, natural yogurt,
store-bought or that
you've made previously
or 1 envelope (about
5 grams) yogurt culture

1 to 4 tablespoons
powdered milk
(optional)

Whether you use the oven or a pressure cooker, you will get lovely, thick yogurt every time. The choice is yours.

OVEN-BAKED **YOGURT**

| Preheat the oven to 125°F (52°C).

| Warm the milk in a pan without heating it above 110°F (44°C). Use a candy thermometer to check the temperature.

| Put the yogurt in a mixing bowl or mixing jug with a pour spout and gradually add the warm milk, stirring with a wooden spoon or rubber spatula.

| Depending on the fat content of the milk and how thick you want the yogurt, add powdered milk and stir well. The more you add, the thicker the yogurt. If you use skim milk, use all 4 tablespoons of powdered milk.

| Pour the yogurt into eight 4-ounce (125-gram) ovenproof pots and set the pots in an ovenproof dish large enough to hold them comfortably.

| Bake the yogurts for 3 hours. Turn off the oven but leave the yogurts in it with the door closed for 5 hours.

| Put lids on the pots or cover them with plastic wrap. Refrigerate for at least 3 hours. The yogurt will keep for 8 to 10 days in the refrigerator.

PRESSURE-COOKED **YOGURT**

| Pour 2 cups plus 2 tablespoons (50 cl) of water into a pressure cooker, clamp down the lid and bring to a boil.

| Warm the milk in a pan without heating it above 110°F (44°C). Use a candy thermometer to check the temperature.

| Put the yogurt in a mixing bowl or mixing jug with a pour spout and gradually add the warm milk, stirring with a wooden spoon or rubber spatula.

| Depending on the fat content of the milk and how thick you want the yogurt, add powdered milk and stir well. The more you add, the thicker the yogurt. If you use skim milk, use all 4 tablespoons of powdered milk.

| Pour the yogurt into eight 4-ounce (125-gram) heat-proof pots. Allow the steam to escape from the pressure cooker and pour the water out. Put the pots inside and clamp down the lid, replacing the valve. Leave overnight.

| In the morning, open the pressure cooker, cover the pots with lids or plastic wrap and refrigerate for at least 3 hours. The yogurt will keep for 8 to 10 days in the refrigerator.

GREEK-STYLE YOGURT

PREPARATION
5 minutes

COOKING
3 to 8 hours

REFRIGERATION
2 to 4 hours

INGREDIENTS

1 quart (1 liter) whole milk

1 envelope (about 5 grams) yogurt culture or 1 cup (225 grams) goat's milk yogurt

Super-creamy Greek yogurt is much easier to make than you might think. The secret is in the draining. Once made, the yogurt keeps for a week. Whole milk results in rich, creamy yogurt.

| In a large saucepan, heat the milk to 110°F (43°C). It's a good idea to use a candy-making or other cooking thermometer to determine the exact temperature. Add the yogurt culture or goat's milk yogurt and stir well.

| Pour the mixture into a large (preferably oven-safe glass) container or into a pressure cooker. Cook the yogurt for 3 hours in the oven or 8 hours in a pressure cooker (see page 19).

| Line a fine-mesh sieve with a piece of muslin or similar cloth and set the sieve over a large bowl. Pour the cooked yogurt onto the cloth and let it drain into the bowl. Put the bowl, with the sieve on it, in the refrigerator for 2 to 4 hours. The yogurt will drain and become thick.

| When the yogurt is as thick as you like it, transfer it to a sealed container or eat it immediately. The yogurt will keep for up to a week in the refrigerator.

GOOD TO KNOW

THE GREEKS LET YOGURT DRAIN FOR UP TO 10 HOURS AT ROOM TEMPERATURE. SOME OF THE GREEK-STYLE YOGURT YOU BUY IN SUPERMARKETS IS BLENDED WITH SOUR CREAM.

★ ★ ★ *Delicious!* ★ ★ ★

CHOCOLATE **PUDDING**

Who could resist the rich, chocolaty taste of this dessert?

| In a bowl, mix the sugar, cocoa powder, and cornstarch. Whisk in the milk and cream until well blended.

| Pour the mixture into a pan and gradually bring to a boil. As soon as it boils, add the chocolate and agar. Let the mixture simmer, stirring constantly, for 3 to 4 minutes or until the mixture thickens.

| Spoon into 4 ramekins and let cool before refrigerating for at least 3 hours. The desserts will keep for up to 1 week in the refrigerator.

MAKES:
FOUR 4- OR 5-OUNCE
(110- TO 150-GRAM)
RAMEKINS

PREPARATION
10 minutes

COOKING
5 minutes

REFRIGERATION
3 hours

INGREDIENTS

⅓ cup (70 grams)
granulated sugar

2 tablespoons
unsweetened cocoa
powder

1 tablespoon cornstarch

1½ cups plus
2 tablespoons (40 cl)
skim milk

7 tablespoons (10 cl)
heavy cream

1 ounce (20 grams)
bittersweet or semisweet
chocolate, coarsely
chopped

Pinch of agar

DON'T BE PUT OFF
BY THE NAME. AGAR IS A
SUBSTANCE EXTRACTED FROM
ALGAE THAT THE JAPANESE HAVE
USED FOR THOUSANDS OF YEARS
AS A NATURAL JELLING AGENT.

ABOUT AGAR

CRÈME **CARAMEL**

MAKES:
6 SERVINGS

PREPARATION
10 minutes

COOKING
10 minutes

REFRIGERATION
3 hours

FOR THE CARAMEL

⅔ cup (100 grams) sugar

1 teaspoon honey

½ teaspoon lemon juice

FOR THE CRÈME

3 cups (70 cl) skim milk

¼ cup (60 grams) granulated sugar

1 tablespoon cornstarch

2 teaspoons pure vanilla extract

1 (2 grams) packet agar

Half the fun of these is inverting the custards and watching the smooth caramel flow over the dessert plate. The tricky bit is making the caramel, but you won't go wrong melting the sugar in a skillet.

TO MAKE THE CARAMEL

| Pour the sugar into a large skillet to make a smooth, uniform layer. Heat over medium heat without mixing or stirring; the sugar will melt and start to caramelize by itself. When this starts to happen, tip the skillet one way and then another to make sure the sugar caramelizes evenly. When it's golden brown, remove from the heat and add the honey and lemon juice. Be very careful and use heavy oven mitts when working with hot sugar.

| Remove the skillet from the heat and let it cool for about 2 minutes. Pour equal amounts of the caramel into each of the six 6- to 8-ounce (170 to 225 grams) ramekins and tip to coat the bottom evenly. Refrigerate while you make the crème caramel.

TO MAKE THE CRÈME

| Put the milk, sugar, cornstarch, vanilla, and agar in a food processor or blender and pulse until well blended. Transfer to a large saucepan and bring to a boil, stirring continuously. Let the mixture bubble gently for 2 minutes while continuing to stir until the mixture thickens.

| Divide the crème evenly among the 6 ramekins. Cover each with plastic wrap or any lids that are provided. Refrigerate for at least 3 hours before serving. The crème caramel will keep in the refrigerator for 3 to 4 days.

CHOCOLATE **MOUSSE**

MAKES:
6 SERVINGS

PREPARATION
20 minutes

COOKING
10 minutes

REFRIGERATION
6 hours

INGREDIENTS
7 ounces (200 grams)
bittersweet or semisweet
chocolate, coarsely
chopped

6 large eggs, preferably
free-range, separated

2 tablespoons salted
butter, cut into small
cubes

Pinch of salt

2 teaspoons
confectioners' sugar

Real French chocolate mousse is made with raw eggs. Here's how.

| Melt the chocolate in the top of a double boiler set over barely simmering water. Stir occasionally. Remove from the heat and set aside to cool until warm.

| Stir the egg yolks into the melted chocolate and then add the butter. Stir or whisk until well blended.

| With a large whisk, beat the egg whites with the salt until stiff. (You might want to use an electric mixer or whisk for this.) Add the sugar and beat until the whites are glistening.

| Stir a third of the meringue into the chocolate mixture until it thins a little. Use a rubber spatula to fold in the remaining meringue. Take care not to deflate the egg whites. Cover the bowl with plastic wrap for at least 6 hours until the mousse is good and firm. The mousse will keep for up to 24 hours in the refrigerator.

NOTE

TO GIVE THE MOUSSE A PERFECTLY SMOOTH TEXTURE, START BEATING THE EGG WHITES WITH A WHISK, BUT FINISH THEM WITH A RUBBER SPATULA.

CREAMY CHOCOLATE MOUSSE

MAKES:
6 SERVINGS

PREPARATION
about 15 minutes

COOKING
about 10 minutes

REFRIGERATION
8 hours

INGREDIENTS
1 sheet gelatin

6 ounces (170 grams) bittersweet or semisweet chocolate, coarsely chopped

½ cup (12.5 cl) whole milk

1 cup (25 cl) chilled heavy cream

Once you master traditional chocolate mousse, why not try making it with whipped cream? So light and deliciously indulgent. See which you prefer...

| Put the gelatin sheet in a bowl with about 1 cup (25 cl) cold water and let it soak for at least 10 minutes.

| Melt the chocolate in the top of a double boiler set over barely simmering water. Stir occasionally until smooth and evenly melted. Remove the top of the double boiler from the heat.

| In a large saucepan, bring the milk to a boil. While it's heating, squeeze the water from the sheet of gelatin. When the milk boils, add the gelatin sheet and stir gently.

| Pour about a third of the milk over the chocolate and stir to incorporate. Add the milk slowly, stirring after each addition until the chocolate mixture is smooth and shiny.

| In a food processor or standing mixer, whip the chilled cream until it doubles in volume and starts to turn dull. It should look like shaving cream.

| Set the top of the double boiler with the chocolate mixture back on the double boiler and heat over medium-high heat for about 5 minutes or until it reaches 110° to 120°F (43° to 49°C). Use a candy thermometer or other cooking thermometer.

| Pour the hot mixture over the whipped cream and blend it gently using a rubber spatula. Don't worry if it seems runny; it will firm up in the refrigerator. Cover the bowl with plastic wrap and refrigerate for at least 8 hours or until firm. The covered mousse will keep for 2 or 3 days in the refrigerator.

SWEET **CHESTNUT** MOUSSE

MAKES:
6 SERVINGS

PREPARATION
about 10 minutes

COOKING
about 1 minute

REFRIGERATION
4 hours

INGREDIENTS
1 sheet gelatin

2 tablespoons milk

¾ cup plus
2 tablespoons
(200 grams) sweet
chestnut purée

¾ cup plus
2 tablespoons (20 cl)
chilled heavy cream

This is a staple of every French childhood. Don't be put off by its appearance, which is a little like grout. Just wait until it sticks to your taste buds. Unforgettable.

| Put the gelatin sheet in a bowl with about 1 cup (25 cl) of cold water and let it soak for at least 10 minutes.

| Put the milk in a small pan and heat it until warm. Squeeze the water from the gelatin and add the gelatin to the pan. Let the gelatin melt and then add the chestnut purée. Stir to mix and then remove the pan from the heat.

| In a food processor or standing mixer, whip the chilled cream until it doubles in volume. Carefully stir the chestnut mixture into the whipped cream. Spoon the mousse into 6 ramekins. Cover with lids or plastic wrap and refrigerate for at least 4 hours until firm. The mousse will keep in the refrigerator for up to 2 days.

NOTE

TO GIVE THE MOUSSE THE
FLAVOR OF COCOA AND CARAMEL,
STIR A PINCH OF CAROB POWDER INTO
THE HEAVY CREAM BEFORE WHIPPING
IT. CAROB POWDER IS A NATURAL
THICKENER AND IS SOLD AT
HEALTH FOOD STORES AND
MANY SUPERMARKETS.
GIVE IT A TRY.

SEMOLINA CAKE WITH **CARAMEL**

MAKES:
6 TO 8 SERVINGS

PREPARATION
about 15 minutes

COOKING
about 15 minutes

REFRIGERATION
4 hours

FOR THE CARAMEL

⅔ cup (100 grams)
sugar

1 teaspoon honey

½ teaspoon lemon juice

FOR THE CAKE

1 vanilla bean

1 quart (1 liter) whole
milk, preferably
organic)

¼ to ⅓ cup (50 to
80 grams) sugar

Pinch of salt

½ cup plus 2
tablespoons (150 grams)
superfine grits

The "real thing" is served in a tin that reminds Frenchmen of Scout camp. We make it in smaller ramekins. Be sure you're at the front of the line when these are served, or there might not be any left.

TO MAKE THE CARAMEL

| Pour the sugar into a large skillet to make a smooth, uniform layer. Heat over medium heat without mixing or stirring; the sugar will melt and start to caramelize by itself. When this starts to happen, tip the skillet one way and then another to make sure the sugar caramelizes evenly. When it's golden brown, remove from the heat and add the honey and lemon juice. Be very careful and use heavy oven mitts when working with hot sugar.

| Let the caramel cool for 2 minutes and then pour it into 6 or 8 lightly oiled ramekins, each 2 to 2½ inches (5 to 6 cm) in diameter. Tip the ramekins so that the caramel coats them evenly. Refrigerate the ramekins while you prepare the grits.

TO MAKE THE CAKE

| Split the vanilla bean lengthwise and using a small, sharp knife, scrape out the seeds.

| Heat the milk, sugar, salt, and vanilla seeds over medium-high heat. As soon as the liquid boils, add the grits. Reduce the heat and simmer for 1 minute, stirring constantly.

| Let the grits cool for a few minutes. Divide them evenly among the ramekins and smooth the surfaces. Let them cool to lukewarm, cover with plastic wrap and refrigerate for at least 4 hours. The semolina cakes will keep in the refrigerator for up to 1 week.

PETITS-SUISSES

You won't have time to wrap paper around these little hunks of fresh cheese to make them look like French petits-suisses. Whether natural or chocolate, they will be devoured as soon as you take them from the fridge.

MAKES:
6 LITTLE CHEESES

PREPARATION
about 10 minutes

RESTING
about 12 hours

REFRIGERATION
10 hours total

INGREDIENTS
1 quart (1 liter) whole milk, preferably organic

2 plain petits-suisses or 4 ounces (125 grams) cream cheese

6 drops rennet

4 ounces (125 grams) sour cream

MAKES:
6 LITTLE CHOCOLATE CHEESES

PREPARATION
about 10 minutes

REFRIGERATION
about 1 hour

INGREDIENTS
6 homemade petits-suisses

1/3 cup (50 grams) confectioners' sugar

1 tablespoon unsweetened cocoa powder

1 teaspoon pure vanilla extract

About 2 tablespoons whey, from the drained cheese curds

NATURAL PETITS-SUISSES

| A day before making the cheeses, heat the milk to 110°F (43°C). Use a candy thermometer or similar cooking thermometer.

| Pour the warm milk into a bowl and add the petits-suisses or cream cheese and the rennet. Cover with plastic wrap and set aside for 12 hours at warm room temperature (68° to 77°F; 20° to 25°C).

| The next day, line a fine-mesh sieve with cheesecloth or a similar clean cloth. Set the sieve over a bowl. Pour the cheese mixture into the sieve and refrigerate. Let the mixture drain into the bowl for 8 hours.

| The curds in the sieve should weigh between 10 and 12 ounces (280 and 330 grams). Add a third of this weight in sour cream to the curds and mix well. (For example, if the curds weigh 12 ounces [330 grams], add 4 ounces [125 grams] of cream cheese.) Reserve the whey (liquid) in the bowl to make the Chocolate Petits-Suisses.

| Spoon the cheese into 6 small pots with fitted lids or cover with plastic wrap and refrigerate for at least 2 hours.

CHOCOLATE PETITS-SUISSES

| In a large bowl, mix the petits-suisses with the confectioners' sugar, cocoa, and vanilla extract. Mix well. Add 1 tablespoon of the whey and stir well. Add more whey to achieve a pleasing consistency, if needed.

| Spoon the cheese mixture into 6 small pots with fitted lids or cover with plastic wrap and refrigerate for at least 1 hour. The chocolate cheeses will keep for 3 to 4 days in the refrigerator.

FONTAINEBLEAU

MAKES:
6 SERVINGS

PREPARATION
5 minutes

REFRIGERATION
8 hours

INGREDIENTS
1 pound (500 grams)
full-fat cream cheese

1 cup (25 cl) chilled
heavy cream

You've heard of the chateau, but Fontainebleau is also famous for this dessert, named for the town. It's an irresistible combination of cream cheese and whipped cream. This is sometimes served with a sprinkling of confectioners' sugar.

| Line a fine-mesh sieve with cheesecloth or a similar clean cloth. Set the sieve over a bowl. Put the cream cheese in the sieve and refrigerate. In a food processor or standing mixer, whip the chilled cream until it doubles in volume. Add the cream cheese to the whipped cream and mix well but gently.

| Pour into 6 ramekins, cover with plastic wrap and refrigerate for at least 6 hours. The Fontainebleau will keep for up to 3 days in the refrigerator.

FOR PERFECT WHIPPED CREAM

❋ USE ONLY HEAVY OR WHIPPING CREAM. DO NOT USE LIGHT CREAM, WHICH WILL NOT WHIP.

❋ MAKE SURE EVERYTHING IS COLD: THE CREAM, THE BOWL AND THE WHIPPING WHISK OR FOOD PROCESSOR BLADE.

❋ DON'T WHIP AT A HIGH SPEED. IT'S BETTER TO WHIP THE CREAM A LITTLE LONGER AT A LOWER SPEED.

❋ ADD THE CONFECTIONERS' SUGAR AT THE VERY END OF MIXING, INCORPORATING IT QUICKLY.

❋ FOR EVERY CUP OF CREAM (25 CL), USE 1 TO 2 TABLESPOONS OF SUGAR.

CONDENSED **MILK**

**MAKES:
ABOUT 1⅓ CUPS
(32 CL)**

PREPARATION
about 5 minutes

COOKING
about 2 minutes

INGREDIENTS
¾ cup (170 grams)
sugar

½ cup plus
2 tablespoons
(160 grams)
powdered milk

Use this in coffee instead of milk and sugar—or simply drink it on its own.

| Put 7 tablespoons (10 cl) of water in a small saucepan and add the sugar. Bring to a boil over medium-high heat and cook until the sugar dissolves. Set aside.

| Let the syrup cool a little and then pour into the bowl of a food processor. Add the powdered milk and mix for 1 to 2 minutes or until smooth.

| Pour into a sterilized jar (see page 140) and set aside to cool. The milk will thicken as it cools. Cover and store in the refrigerator for up to 3 weeks.

NOTE

IF YOU BOIL THE SUGAR IN MILK INSTEAD OF WATER, IT'S LIKELY YOU WILL WIND UP WITH MILK-FLAVORED JAM. THERE'S NO SUCH DANGER WITH POWDERED MILK.

STRAWBERRY **SMOOTHIES**

These tasty drinks fill you with energy!

PREPARATION
5 minutes

COOKING
3 to 8 hours

REFRIGERATION
3 hours

INGREDIENTS
3 ⅓ cups (80 cl) whole, low-fat or skim milk

½ cup (125 grams) plain, natural yogurt, store-bought, or that you've made previously or 1 envelope (about 5 grams) yogurt culture

4 tablespoons (6 cl) strawberry or raspberry syrup

VANILLA SUGAR IS EASY TO MAKE

BURY A VANILLA BEAN IN A CUP (170 G) OF GRANULATED SUGAR. FOR MORE SUGAR, ADD ANOTHER BEAN OR TWO. THE BEANS CAN BE WHOLE OR SPLIT IN HALF. EVEN THE PODS WITH THE BEANS SCRAPED OUT WILL PERFUME THE SUGAR. COVER TIGHTLY AND SET ASIDE FOR A DAY OR TWO BEFORE USING. USE THE SUGAR TO FLAVOR DESSERTS, DRINKS AND ANYTHING ELSE YOU LIKE. A TABLESPOON OF SUGAR HAS ABOUT THE SAME FLAVORING POWER AS HALF A TEASPOON OF VANILLA EXTRACT. VANILLA SUGAR KEEP FOR ABOUT 6 MONTHS.

| Warm the milk in a pan without heating it above 110°F (43°C). Use a candy thermometer to check the temperature.

| Put the yogurt in a mixing bowl or mixing jug with a pour spout and gradually add the warm milk, stirring with a wooden spoon or rubber spatula. Stir in the strawberry or raspberry syrup.

| Pour the yogurt into 6 oven-proof pots and set the pots in an oven-proof dish large enough to hold them comfortably.

| Bake the yogurts for 3 hours. Turn off the oven but leave the yogurts in it with the door closed for 5 hours.

| Put lids on the pots or cover them with plastic wrap. Shake well to make drinkable. Refrigerate for at least 3 hours. The yogurt will keep for 8 to 10 days in the refrigerator.

TO MAKE A VANILLA SMOOTHIE

Follow the recipe above. Split a vanilla bean in half and scrape the seeds into the milk. (If you don't have a vanilla bean, use 1 teaspoon of pure vanilla extract.) Add 2 tablespoons of sugar and ¼ teaspoon of vanilla sugar, if using.

Heat the milk as directed to around 110°F (43°C), stirring so that the sugar dissolves. Proceed with the recipe as instructed.

TO MAKE PRESSURE-COOKED YOGURT

| Pour 2 cups plus 2 tablespoons (50 cl) of water into a pressure cooker, clamp down the lid, and bring to a boil.

| Warm the milk in a pan without heating it above 110°F (43°C). Use a candy thermometer to check the temperature.

| Put the yogurt in a mixing bowl or mixing jug with a pour spout and gradually add the warm milk, stirring with a wooden spoon or rubber spatula.

| Pour the yogurt into 6 heat-proof pots. Allow the steam to escape from the pressure cooker and pour the water out. Put the pots inside and clamp down the lid, replacing the valve. Leave overnight.

| In the morning, open the pressure cooker, cover the pots with lids or plastic wrap, and shake well to make drinkable. Refrigerate for at least 3 hours. The yogurt will keep for 8 to 10 days in the refrigerator.

PRETZEL STICKS

These crunchy sticks are easier to make than shaped pretzels—and they're lightly flavored with beer (in place of malt, which is the traditional flavoring).

MAKES:
ABOUT 60
PRETZELS

PREPARATION
about 15 minutes

RESTING
about 1 hour

COOKING
about 20 minutes

INGREDIENTS
1 teaspoon active dry yeast

1 tablespoon lager beer

2 cups (250 grams) all-purpose flour

1 teaspoon sugar

1 teaspoon table salt

2 teaspoons baking soda

About 2 teaspoons sea salt

NOTE
YOU CAN SPRINKLE FLAVORINGS OTHER THAN SALT ON THE THE PRETZELS. TRY PAPRIKA, SESAME SEEDS, POPPY SEEDS...

| Dissolve the yeast in 6 tablespoons (9 cl) of warm water. Stir to mix and then stir in the beer.

| In a mixing bowl, mix together the flour, sugar, and table salt. Make a hollow in the center and add the yeast mixture. Mix with a wooden spoon until the liquid is absorbed.

| Turn the dough out on a lightly floured surface and knead for about 10 minutes or until no longer sticky. Alternatively, you can use a bread machine or standing mixer with a dough hook. Return the dough to the bowl, cover with a damp dishtowel or similar cloth, and let it rise in a warm, draft-free place for about 1 hour.

| Preheat the oven to 400°F (200°C).

| Lift the dough from the bowl and drop it on a lightly floured work surface to expel the air. Divide it into 4 equal sections and roll each into a roll about 4¾ inches long (12 cm) and ⅛ inch thick (4 mm). Using a pizza wheel or very sharp knife, cut the rolls lengthwise into very thin pieces (less then ⅛ inch or 2 mm, if possible).

| Fill a large saucepan with water, add the baking soda, and bring to a boil. Drop the pretzel sticks in the boiling water and cook for 30 seconds. Lift them from the water with a slotted spoon or similar tool and lay them on a dry dishcloth to drain.

| Transfer the pretzel sticks on a baking tray lined with parchment paper, sprinkle liberally with sea salt and then bake them for 12 to 15 minutes or until golden brown. Keep a close eye on them; the thinner they are, the more easily they will burn.

| Remove them from the oven and let them cool. The pretzels will keep in an airtight tin for up to 3 days.

SWISS CHEESE **CRACKERS**

You can make finer, crunchier cheese squares than any you can buy. Rolling them paper thin takes some practice, but it's well worth the effort.

MAKES: ABOUT 120 CRACKERS

PREPARATION
about 10 minutes

FREEZING
about 1 hour

COOKING
about 5 minutes

INGREDIENTS
½ cup (70 grams) all-purpose flour

2 pinches salt

Pinch of sugar

Pinch of baking powder or Homemade Chemical Leavener (page 40)

⅓ cup (70 grams) grated Swiss cheese

2 tablespoons butter, cut into cubes

| In a mixing bowl, mix together the flour, salt, sugar, and leavener (baking powder). Add the cheese and cubes of butter and work the mixture with your fingertips until it's crumbly. Add 1 tablespoon of cold water and mix until the dough comes together in a ball. You may need to add a second tablespoon of cold water.

| Divide the dough into 2 equal parts and put each one in a sturdy plastic bag. Working through the bag, divide each lump of pastry into a bar with a squared cross section. Use a ruler to help if necessary. Freeze for at least 1 hour.

| Preheat the oven to 400°F (200°C).

| Cut each bar lengthways in half and then cut each in half again. You will have 8 thin, squared rods. Lay the rods on a sheet of parchment paper or silicone baking mat. Cover with parchment paper or another mat and, using a rolling pin, roll the rods into a very thin sheet of pastry. Lift off the parchment paper and using a sharp knife, score the sheets of pastry into 1-inch (2.5 cm) squares. Lift the scored pastry, still on the parchment paper, directly on a baking sheet. Bake for about 5 minutes until the pastry squares are lightly golden around the edges.

| Let the pastry sheet cool on a wire rack, still on the parchment paper. When cool, break into crackers and store in an airtight tin for up to 5 days.

CRACKERS

These salty crackers are a breeze to make. Be sure to roll the dough wafer thin so that the baked crackers explode in your mouth.

| In a mixing bowl, mix together the flour, sugar, salt, and leavener. Add the egg, oil, and 2 teaspoons of water. Mix for 1 to 2 minutes until the dough is smooth. Cover the bowl with plastic wrap and refrigerate for at least 30 minutes.

| Preheat the oven to 350°F (180°C).

| Take the dough from the refrigerator and roll it on a lightly floured surface into a large, very thin rectangle (about ⅛ inch [3 mm]). Using a pizza wheel, cut out rectangles measuring about 2½ inches (6 cm) long by 1¾ inches (4 cm).

| Lay the rectangles on a baking pan lined with parchment paper and prick each one 5 or 6 times with a fork. Dust the crackers with salt.

| Bake for about 10 minutes until the crackers are lightly golden brown around the edges. Let the crackers cool on wire racks. They will crisp up as they cool and will keep for up to 1 week in an airtight container.

HOMEMADE CHEMICAL LEAVENER

This is easy to make and very inexpensive. Substitute baking powder for it, if you prefer.

| Mix all the ingredients in a bowl. Use a level teaspoon of baking soda for every 2 cups (250 grams) of flour.

| Store in a tightly lidded glass jar or tin. The leavener will keep for up to 1 year. To test if the leavener is active, drop a pinch in a little water; it should fizz slightly.

NOTE

THIS IS ALSO CALLED BAKING POWDER, A MIXTURE OF AN ALKALINE (BAKING SODA) AND AN ACID (CREAM OF TARTAR) THAT, WHEN ADDED TO LIQUID, FORMS CARBON DIOXIDE, WHICH LETS THE BAKED GOOD RISE AND GIVES IT ITS TEXTURE.

MAKES: ABOUT 30 CRACKERS

PREPARATION
about 20 minutes

REFRIGERATION
at least 30 minutes

COOKING
about 10 minutes

INGREDIENTS
1¾ cups (200 grams) all-purpose flour

1 tablespoon sugar

1 teaspoon table salt, plus more for dusting

2 pinches baking powder or Homemade Chemical Leavener

1 large egg, lightly beaten

1 tablespoon plus 1 teaspoon sunflower, peanut, or canola oil

---

MAKES: ABOUT ½ CUP (4 GRAMS)

PREPARATION
about 5 minutes

INGREDIENTS
¼ cup (50 grams) cream of tartar

2 tablespoons baking soda

2 tablespoons (25 grams) cornstarch

PARTY **TRIANGLES**

**MAKES:
65 TO 70 CRACKERS**

PREPARATION
about 15 minutes

REFRIGERATION
at least 1 hour

COOKING
15 to 20 minutes

RESTING
about 1 hour

INGREDIENTS
1 cup plus
2 tablespoons
(180 grams) all-purpose
flour

4 teaspoons cornstarch

1 tablespoon sugar

¼ teaspoon baking
powder or Homemade
Chemical Leavener,
page 40

¼ teaspoon table salt

1 tablespoon sesame
seeds

1 tablespoon poppy
seeds

6 tablespoons
(70 grams) butter, cut
into cubes

4 teaspoons poppy seed
oil or peanut oil

These crispy crackers are flavored with sesame and poppy seeds and so good, you won't want to share them.

| In a mixing bowl, mix together the flour, cornstarch, sugar, baking powder or leavener, salt, and sesame and poppy seeds. Add the butter cubes and the oil.

| Work the dough into a crumble with your fingertips. Gradually add 4 teaspoons of cold water to make a ball. Wrap the ball of dough in plastic wrap and refrigerate for at least 1 hour.

| Preheat the oven to 350°F (180°C).

| Unwrap the ball of dough and gently spread it on a large sheet of parchment paper or a silicone mat. Top with another sheet of parchment or silicone mat. Use rolling pin to flatten it as thin as possible.

| Using a pizza wheel or sharp knife, cut the pastry into long strips that are about 1¼ inches (3 cm) wide. Cut these strips into triangles by scoring the strips with back-and-forth diagonal cuts.

| Lift the bottom parchment paper or silicone mat and put it on a baking sheet. Bake for 15 to 20 minutes, or until the crackers are lightly golden. Turn off the oven and wedge the door open with a wooden spoon or similar tool and let the crackers dry in the oven for about 1 hour or until they are very crunchy—as crunchy as possible. The crackers will keep for up to 1 week in an airtight tin.

NOTE

POPPY SEED OIL IS SOLD IN NATURAL FOOD AND SPECIALTY SHOPS. IT WILL ENHANCE THE FLAVOR OF THE CRACKERS MORE THAN PEANUT OIL, WHICH IS A DECENT SUBSTITUTION.

DÉLICE MAISON
ORIGINAL · UNIQUE
À CONSOMMER AVANT

ITALIAN **BREAD** STICKS

These crunchy bread sticks never seem long enough. How can you make them long and thin? Slice the dough with a pizza wheel.

**MAKES:
ABOUT 40
BREADSTICKS**

PREPARATION
about 15 minutes

RESTING
1 hour 30 minutes

COOKING
about 15 minutes

INGREDIENTS
½ packet active dry yeast (each packet weighs ¼ ounce; 7 grams)

¾ cup (125 grams) all-purpose flour plus a little for dusting

¾ cup (125 grams) fine wheat semolina

2 teaspoons sugar

½ teaspoon salt

2 teaspoons olive oil

A few pinches dried thyme or oregano, freeze-dried garlic, cayenne pepper, cumin seeds, or aniseed, optional

Sea salt, for dusting

| Dissolve the yeast in about ½ cup (12.5 cl) of warm water.

| In a mixing bowl, mix the flour, semolina, sugar, and salt. Make a well in the middle of the flour and pour in the dissolved yeast and then the oil. Using your hands or a wooden spoon, mix the dough until it comes together. Turn it out onto a lightly floured surface and knead for about 10 minutes, until it stops sticking to your fingers. Add a few pinches of herbs or spices, if desired, and mix into the dough. Return the dough to the bowl and cover with a damp dishtowel or similar cloth and let it rise for 1 hour in a warm, dry place.

| Once the dough has doubled in volume, knead it a little and then spread it out on a floured board in a rectangle about ¼ inch (½ mm) thick. Cover it again and let it rest for about 30 minutes longer.

| Heat the oven to 350°F (180°C).

| Using a pizza wheel, slice the dough into strings around ¼ inch (½ mm) thick and 8 inches (20 cm) long. Stretch them to make them even finer, and lay them on a baking sheet lined with parchment paper.

| Sprinkle the bread sticks with sea salt and bake for about 15 minutes. The thinner the bread sticks are, the faster they'll cook, so watch them carefully to make sure they don't burn. Let them cool on wire racks before serving.

| The bread sticks will keep in an airtight tin for up to 1 week (if there are any left!).

BLINIS & DIPS
(HUMMUS, TAPENADE & EGGPLANT PÂTÉ)

Once you taste these super-simple blinis, those you buy in plastic packages will seem like lumps. Making the dips to go with the blinis is just as easy.

HUMMUS

| In the bowl of a food processor fitted with a metal blade, combine the drained beans, sesame paste, olive oil, lemon juice, and garlic. Pulse several times until smooth. Season to taste with salt and pepper and pulse a few more times.

| Transfer to a bowl and cover with plastic wrap. Refrigerate for at least 1 hour before serving. The hummus will keep in the refrigerator for up to 5 days if well covered.

TAPENADE

| In the bowl of a food processor fitted with a metal blade, combine the olives, capers, anchovy fillets, herbes de Provence, olive oil, and brandy. Pulse several times until smooth. If the tapenade is too thick, add a little water.

| Transfer to a bowl and cover with plastic wrap. Refrigerate for at least 1 hour before serving. The tapenade will keep in the refrigerator for up to 2 weeks if lightly coated with olive oil and well covered.

**MAKES:
ABOUT 1 CUP**

PREPARATION
about 5 minutes

REFRIGERATION
1 hour

INGREDIENTS
1 can (15.5 ounces, 425 grams) garbonzo beans in water, drained

4 teaspoons sesame paste

4 teaspoons olive oil

Juice of ½ lemon

1 clove garlic

Salt and freshly ground pepper

**MAKES:
ABOUT 1 CUP**

PREPARATION
about 5 minutes

REFRIGERATION
1 hour

INGREDIENTS
1 cup (225 grams) pitted black olives

¼ cup (50 grams) capers, packed in salt water or vinegar, rinsed well

6 anchovy fillets, packed in oil

2 teaspoons dried herbes de Provence

2 teaspoons olive oil

1 teaspoon brandy

QUICK EGGPLANT PÂTÉ

MAKES:
ABOUT 2 CUPS

PREPARATION
about 10 minutes

COOKING
5 minutes

INGREDIENTS
2 fresh, shiny eggplants

½ cup (125 grams) sheep's milk plain yogurt

Juice of ¼ lemon

2 tablespoons olive oil

Salt and freshly ground pepper

Sesame seeds, for garnish

| Peel the eggplants and cut them into cubes. Transfer to a boil and add 2 teaspoons of water. Microwave on High for 5 minutes.

| Put the softened eggplant in the bowl of a food processor fitted with the metal blade. Add the yogurt, lemon juice, and olive oil and process until smooth. Add salt and pepper to taste and pulse a few times.

| Transfer to a bowl and cover with plastic wrap. Refrigerate for at least 1 hour. Sprinkle with sesame seeds before serving. The paté will keep in the refrigerator for up to 5 days if well covered.

SUPER-SIMPLE BLINIS

MAKES:
8 BLINIS

PREPARATION
about 5 minutes

COOKING
about 15 minutes

INGREDIENTS
½ cup (125 grams) whole milk, plain natural yogurt

1 large egg

1 cup (150 grams) all-purpose flour

2 teaspoons Homemade Chemical Leavener (page 40) or baking powder

2 pinches salt

Flavorless oil, for the pan

| In a mixing bowl, whisk the yogurt and egg together. Add the flour, leavener, and salt. Stir well.

| Lightly oil a skillet and set over medium heat. When hot, drop 4 small tablespoons of the batter into the pan. Leave plenty of space between them. Cook until bubbles appear on the surface of the blinis. Turn over and cook for 45 seconds longer. Lift the cooked blinis from the skillet and set aside on a plate. Continue with the remaining batter, making 4 more blinis.

| Let the blinis cool before serving with the dips. They will keep in the freezer for up to 1 month (if you don't eat them right away!).

POPCORN

MAKES:
1 SMALL BOWL

PREPARATION
2 to 3 minutes

COOKING
5 to 10 minutes

INGREDIENTS
2 teaspoons sunflower, corn, or canola oil

½ cup (100 grams) popping corn

Salt

For your very own movie night, feather-light popcorn is easy to make. Flavor it any way you like.

| Heat the oil in a large, heavy skillet with a lid over medium-high heat until hot. Check the temperature by dropping a single kernel of corn in the skillet; if it pops, the oil is hot.

| Pour the rest of the kernels into the pan, spreading them evenly over the surface. Cover immediately with the lid and shake the pan from side to side so that the kernels heat evenly and all of them pop. Be sure you hold the lid firmly in place. When the popping becomes intermittent, remove the pan from the heat.

| Season to taste with salt and serve immediately, or flavor the popcorn with one of the following flavoring mixtures.

| The salted and vanilla popcorn will keep for up to 2 days in an airtight container. The caramel popcorn will keep for up to 24 hours if kept in an airtight container (any longer, and the popcorn goes soft).

BARBECUE, PIZZA, OR CURRY FLAVOR

Mix the spices or seasoning and the salt with the melted butter or oil, drizzle over the popped corn and mix by hand.

CARAMEL FLAVOR

Drizzle the hot caramel over the popped corn and mix with a spatula.

VANILLA FLAVOR

Mix the vanilla sugar and the melted butter, drizzle over the popped corn and mix by hand.

BARBECUE FLAVOR

½ teaspoon paprika

¼ teaspoon dried garlic

¼ teaspoon chili powder

4 tablespoons (50 grams) butter, melted

PIZZA FLAVOR

2 teaspoons tomato puree

1 teaspoon dried oregano

2 teaspoons grated parmesan

¼ teaspoon salt

2 tablespoons olive oil

CURRY FLAVOR

2 teaspoons curry powder

4 teaspoons grated coconut

4 tablespoons (50 grams) butter, melted

SWEET POPCORN:

CARAMEL FLAVOR

See crème caramel recipe on page 24

VANILLA FLAVOR

4 tablespoons (60 grams) vanilla sugar (see page 36)

4 tablespoons (50 grams) butter, melted

CHEESE STICKS

With just five ingredients on hand, you'll never need to buy crunchy cheese sticks again.

**MAKES:
ABOUT 30 CHEESE
STICKS**

PREPARATION
about 10 minutes

REFRIGERATION
at least 2 hours

COOKING
10 to 12 minutes

INGREDIENTS
1 cup (150 grams)
all-purpose flour

½ teaspoon turmeric

½ teaspoon mustard
powder

½ cup (100 grams)
salted butter, cut into
cubes

4 ounces (100 grams)
Swiss or cheddar
cheese, grated

| In a large mixing bowl, whisk the flour with the turmeric and mustard. Add the cubes of butter and using your fingers, work into the flour until it is crumbly.

| Mix the grated cheese into the flour and press into a ball. If it won't hold together, add a few drops of cold water. Wrap in plastic wrap and refrigerate for at least 2 hours until firm.

| Preheat the oven to 350°F (180°C).

| Break off teaspoon-size pieces of the cold dough and roll between your palms into sticks measuring 1 to 1¼ inches (2.5 to 3 cm) long.

| Lay the cheese sticks on a baking sheet lined with parchment paper. Bake for 10 to 12 minutes or until the sticks are lightly golden. Let the cheese sticks cool on the sheets for a few moments before transferring them to wire racks to cool completely.

| The cheese sticks will keep for up to 5 days if stored in an airtight tin.

TO MAKE THE CHEESE STICKS EVEN
CRUNCHIER, SPRINKLE THEM WITH SESAME OR
POPPY SEEDS BEFORE BAKING. TO MAKE THEM
MORE GOLDEN BROWN, BRUSH THEM WITH
WHISKED EGG YOLKS BEFORE BAKING.

★★★ TIP ★★★

TORTILLA **CHIPS**

Make your own tortillas and then turn the tortillas into chips perfect for dipping in guacamole (page 66). To make life easier, begin with store-bought tortillas and then fry them to make chips.

**MAKES:
ABOUT 11 OUNCES
(300 GRAMS)**

PREPARATION
about 20 minutes

STANDING TIME
30 minutes

COOKING
30 minutes

INGREDIENTS
½ cup plus 2 tablespoons (15 cl) milk

¾ cup plus 1 tablespoon (125 grams) bread flour (plus a little for rolling)

¾ cup plus 1 tablespoon (125 grams) stoneground yellow cornmeal

2 teaspoons sugar

2 teaspoons Homemade Chemical Leavener (page 40) or baking powder

¼ teaspoon salt (plus a little for flavoring)

2 teaspoons sunflower or canola oil

1 quart (1 liter) peanut or grapeseed oil, for frying

1 teaspoon mild paprika

½ teaspoon cumin

| Warm the milk in a saucepan over medium-high heat.

| In a mixing bowl, mix the flour and cornmeal with the sugar, leavener, and salt. Make a well in the middle and add the warm milk and 2 teaspoons of oil. Mix well and knead the dough for 2 to 3 minutes. Alternatively, use a mixer or bread machine. Wrap the dough in plastic wrap and let it rest for 30 minutes at room temperature.

| Divide the dough into 6 or 8 pieces (according to the size of your skillet). Roll them by hand into balls and then flatten the balls into thin circles about 8 inches (20 cm) in diameter. As you do so, regularly turn them and dust them with flour so that they don't stick.

| Heat a lightly oiled heavy skillet (preferably cast-iron) or a large, flat griddle and fry each tortilla over high heat for about 45 seconds on each side

| In a large, heavy pot or deep skillet heat the peanut or grapeseed oil over medium-high heat until very hot.

| Meanwhile, cut the tortillas into triangles with scissors and drop them, a handful at a time, into hot oil. When they're good and golden, after 2 to 3 minutes, lift them from the oil with long-handled tongs or a slotted spoon and drain on paper towels. Sprinkle with salt, paprika, and cumin.

| Repeat with the remaining tortillas. Let the oil regain its heat between batches. The chips will keep for a week in an airtight container.

OLD-FASHIONED
POTATO CHIPS

MAKES:
ABOUT 9 OUNCES
(250 GRAMS)

PREPARATION
about 20 minutes

COOKING
about 25 minutes

INGREDIENTS
2 pounds 3 ounces
(1 kg) floury potatoes,
such as russets, washed
and peeled

2 quarts (2 liters)
grapeseed or peanut
oil, for frying

1 teaspoon salt

This is how potato chips used to be made. Those little bags didn't appear until the 1950s.

| Slice the potatoes about ¼-inch (1-mm) thick using a grater or slicer.

| Rinse the slices thoroughly in cold water until the water turns cloudy. Carefully dry the potato slices with a clean dishtowel or similar cloth. Spread them out to air dry, too. They must be completely dry, or they won't be crispy.

| In a deep pan or deep fryer, heat the oil over medium-high heat until it reaches about 325°F (165°C) (use a cooking or frying thermometer). To test if the oil is hot enough, drop a single slice into the oil; if tiny bubbles appear on both sides, you're ready to go.

| Drop the potato slices by the handful into the hot oil and stir them about with a metal whisk so that they don't stick together. Let them fry for about 5 minutes or until they're golden and have stopped crackling.

| Lift the potato chips from the hot oil with long-handled tongs or a slotted spoon and let them drain on paper towels. Season with a few pinches of salt.

| Repeat with the remaining chips. Let the oil regain its heat between batches. The chips will keep for 2 days in a paper bag or tin.

NOTE

TO CRISP THE CHIPS UP THE DAY AFTER THEY ARE FRIED, MICROWAVE THEM FOR A FEW SECONDS, OR LEAVE THEM FOR A FEW MINUTES IN A HOT, 350°F (180°C) OVEN THAT HAS BEEN TURNED OFF.

BURGER MEAL

Everything's homemade here, even the ketchup!

MAKES: 4 BURGERS

PREPARATION
about 5 minutes

COOKING
2 to 3 minutes

INGREDIENTS
1 large red onion
½ bunch flat-leaf parsley
12 ounces (350 grams) ground beef
4 teaspoons plain Homemade Breadcrumbs (see page 64)
2 teaspoons prepared mustard
2 teaspoons Worcestershire sauce
½ teaspoon dried thyme
Sugar, salt, and freshly ground black pepper

BURGERS

| Peel and finely chop the onion. Finely chop the parsley.

| In a mixing bowl, mix the ground beef with the onions and parsley, breadcrumbs, mustard, Worcestershire sauce, and thyme. Form into 4 burgers and refrigerate until needed.

| Just before cooking, season the burgers on both sides with small pinches of sugar and salt and a grinding of pepper.

| Fry or grill the burgers for 2 to 3 minutes on each side, or longer, depending on how thick they are and how well done you like them.

MAKES: 4 BUNS

PREPARATION
about 30 minutes

STANDING TIME
about 1 hour and 30 minutes

COOKING
about 20 minutes

INGREDIENTS
½ packet active dry yeast (each packet weighs 1¼ ounces)
½ cup (12.5 cl) warm skim milk plus a little for brushing on the buns
2 cups (250 grams) bread flour
2 level teaspoons sugar
½ teaspoon salt
2 tablespoons butter, cubed and softened
Sesame or poppy seeds, for sprinkling

BUNS

| Dissolve the yeast in warm milk.

| In a mixing bowl, mix the flour with the sugar and salt. Make a hollow in the middle and add the yeast mixture. Mix with a wooden spoon and then knead the dough for about 10 minutes on a lightly floured surface until it's smooth. Work the butter into the bread dough and form into a rounded shape. Put the dough in the bowl, cover with a damp dishtowel or similar cloth, and let rise for 30 minutes at room temperature.

| Punch down the dough to release the air and divide into 4 equal pieces. Roll each piece into balls and brush each with a little milk.

| Spread the sesame seeds or poppy seeds on a plate and then roll the dough in them to coat. Put the coated balls of dough on a baking sheet, cover with the damp cloth again, and let the buns rise for a further 1 hour.

| Preheat the oven to 400°F (200°C).

| Remove the cloth and bake the buns, still on the baking sheet, for about 20 minutes or until the buns have fully expanded and turned golden brown.

MAKES:
2 10-OUNCE
BOTTLES (280 GRAMS)

PREPARATION
about 15 minutes

COOKING
1 hour 35 minutes

INGREDIENTS
2¼ pounds (1 kg) ripe
tomatoes

1 stalk celery

1 onion

1 clove garlic

2 teaspoons olive oil

1 bay leaf

1 sprig thyme

1 sprig rosemary

1 teaspoon salt

¾ cup (18 cl) red wine
vinegar

½ cup plus 2 tablespoons
(150 grams) sugar

2 pinches each of
cayenne pepper, ground
nutmeg, ground ginger,
ground coriander, ground
clove

¼ teaspoon pepper

KETCHUP

| Wash the tomatoes, remove the stems, and cut them into pieces.

| Peel and chop the celery and onion and slice the garlic clove.

| Pour the oil into a large, deep pot and gently cook the onion, garlic, celery, and tomato over medium heat. Add the bay leaf, thyme, rosemary, and salt. Simmer for 30 minutes, stirring frequently.

| Remove the herbs from the ketchup and stir again. Strain the ketchup through a sieve into a bowl. Add the vinegar, sugar, cayenne, nutmeg, ginger, coriander, and clove. Season with pepper.

| Return the ketchup to the pot and simmer for 1 hour longer, stirring frequently, until the mixture thickens like jam.

| While it's still hot, pour the ketchup into sterilized bottles or jars. The ketchup will keep for 1 week in an unsterilized bottle or similar container in the refrigerator. It can be frozen for up to a year, and if stored in sterilized bottles and properly sealed, will keep for a year. (For more on sterilizing jars, see page 140).

PUTTING IT ALL TOGETHER

| Cut the buns in half crosswise.

| Spread the ketchup on one side of the buns and mustard (see page 73) on the other. Top with a burger and garnish with lettuce, pickles, sliced tomatoes, cheese, bacon, etc., to order.

FOR A CHEESEBURGER
PUT CHEESE ON THE BURGER 1 MINUTE BEFORE IT'S FULLY COOKED. THIS WAY THE CHEESE MELTS JUST THE RIGHT AMOUNT.

SPICY **POTATO** WEDGES

While they're cooking, you can do something else— no need for takeout.

| Preheat the oven to 400°F (200°C).

| Thoroughly wash the potatoes and cut into wedge-shaped quarters, without peeling them. Dry them carefully and lay them in a single layer in a large oven dish.

| Put the oil in a bowl and add the garlic, flour, sugar, thyme, turmeric, paprika, and salt. Mix well and pour over the potato wedges. Using your hands, make sure each wedge is completely coated.

| Bake for about 45 minutes or until the wedges are browned and cooked through. Turn them 3 or 4 times during baking.

| These do not keep. The potato wedges must be eaten immediately!

NOTE

TO ENSURE THE WEDGES ARE FULLY COATED WITH OIL AND FLAVORINGS WITHOUT GETTING YOUR HANDS MESSY, PUT EVERYTHING IN A TIGHTLY CLOSED PLASTIC CONTAINER AND GIVE IT A GOOD SHAKE.

CHICKEN **NUGGETS**

You will taste the difference right away when you use real chicken instead of chopped scraps.

MAKES:
4 TO 6 SERVINGS

PREPARATION
about 15 minutes

COOKING
8 to 10 minutes

INGREDIENTS
⅓ cup (50 grams)
all-purpose flour

1 teaspoon paprika

Salt and freshly ground
pepper

3 large egg whites,
preferably free-range

4 boneless, skinless
chicken breasts,
preferably organic

3½ cups (150 grams)
corn flakes, lightly
crushed

7 tablespoons
(10 cl) grapeseed or
sunflower oil

| Mix the flour and paprika in a shallow dish and season generously with salt and pepper.

| In a bowl, beat the egg whites lightly with a fork and set aside.

| Cut the chicken breast into cubes about 2 inch (5 cm) square. Toss them in the flour mixture to coat and then dip them in the egg white. Finally, toss them with the corn flakes, pressing the flakes gently into the coating so they stick.

| Heat the oil in a deep frying pan and when hot, cook the chicken for 4 to 5 minutes on each side until golden and cooked through. Be sure they do not burn.

| Drain the chicken on paper towels and serve hot with Homemade Barbecue Sauce (page 78) or Homemade Ketchup (see page 55).

NOTE

FOR FAT-FREE NUGGETS,
BAKE THEM FOR 25 MINUTES
AT 350°F (180°C), TURNING
THEM HALFWAY
THROUGH.

POTATO BALLS

These little potato bombs will explode when you bite into them. And they are easier to make than you might think.

MAKES: 4 SERVINGS

PREPARATION
about 20 minutes

STANDING TIME
5 minutes

COOKING
about 10 minutes

INGREDIENTS

9 ounces (250 grams) or 2 packets dried potato flakes, preferably organic

3 cups (70 cl) milk

¼ teaspoon ground nutmeg

Salt and freshly ground pepper

2 large eggs, preferably free-range

1 cup (60 grams) Homemade Breadcrumbs (see page 64)

Sunflower oil, for frying, or another good frying oil

| In a mixing bowl, mix the potato flakes with the milk and nutmeg and season with salt and pepper. Add 1 egg and 1 egg yolk (keep the egg white for coating the balls) and stir to mix. Let the mixture swell for 5 minutes.

| With a spoon, scoop out about 1 tablespoon of the mixture at a time and roll them into balls with your hands.

| Pour the breadcrumbs into a shallow dish or plate and put the reserved egg white in a small bowl. Dip the potato balls in the egg white before rolling them in the breadcrumbs.

| Pour the oil into a large, deep frying pan to a depth of 1¼ inches (3 cm) and put it over high heat. When the oil is hot, fry half the potato balls for about 4 minutes until golden.

| Drain on paper towels while you let the oil regain its heat. When the oil is hot, fry the remaining balls.

| If you can't serve the balls immediately, hold them in the oven at 200°F (93°C) to keep them crisp. The potato balls will keep for 2 days in the refrigerator if stored in an airtight container. Refrigerate the balls before coating in breadcrumbs. Coat them right before frying.

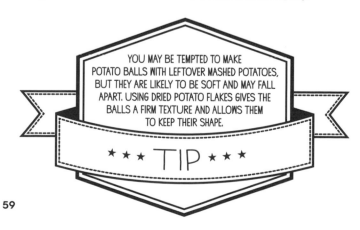

YOU MAY BE TEMPTED TO MAKE POTATO BALLS WITH LEFTOVER MASHED POTATOES, BUT THEY ARE LIKELY TO BE SOFT AND MAY FALL APART. USING DRIED POTATO FLAKES GIVES THE BALLS A FIRM TEXTURE AND ALLOWS THEM TO KEEP THEIR SHAPE.

★ ★ ★ TIP ★ ★ ★

CORDON BLEU

No one knows why the French call these "cordon bleu"— possibly because the taste warrants a blue ribbon or for the blue string sometimes used to hold them together while they're cooking. What is certain is that they are delicious.

MAKES:
4 SERVINGS

PREPARATION
about 20 minutes

COOKING
15 to 20 minutes

INGREDIENTS
2 turkey breast scallops (fillets)

6 ounces (175 grams) firm cheese, such as cheddar or Swiss

2 thin slices ham

1 large egg

4 teaspoons milk

Grated nutmeg

Salt and pepper

4 teaspoons all-purpose flour

2 cups (100 grams) Homemade Breadcrumbs (see page 64)

2 tablespoons vegetable oil, for frying

| Slice the scallops in half lengthwise so that they are twice as thin as they were. Use a rolling pin or the back of a small frying pan to pound the turkey so that it's even thinner. (You can ask the butcher to do this.)

| Grate the cheese into thin slices and cut the slices of ham in half.

| In a small bowl, beat the egg with the milk, a little nutmeg, salt and pepper.

| Lay 1 slice of ham on each turkey scallop. Cover half of the ham with a slice or two of cheese. Take care not to put the cheese all the way to the edges, so that it doesn't ooze out when the scallops are cooked. Fold the scallop in half and roll it in the flour, making sure the edges are well coated. Finally, coat in the egg mixture and the breadcrumbs.

| Preheat the oven to 350°F (180°C).

| Heat the oil in a deep frying pan and when hot, fry the scallops for 2 minutes each side, turning them frequently to prevent burning. Alternatively, put the scallops directly into a very hot skillet and cook 2 minutes each side. Bake for 10 minutes until cooked through.

| Eat immediately!

HOMEMADE PIZZA

Forget frozen pizza. Homemade pizzas are the real deal. Choose your favorite toppings.

MAKES:
4 SERVINGS

PREPARATION
about 25 minutes

COOKING
10 to 15 minutes

PIZZA DOUGH
INGREDIENTS

1 packet active dry yeast (each packet weighs 1¼ ounces)

1 teaspoon honey

1 tablespoon olive oil

1¾ cups (220 grams) unbleached all-purpose flour

½ teaspoon salt

TOMATO SAUCE
INGREDIENTS

½ cup plus 2 tablespoons (15 cl) tomato puree

1 garlic clove, crushed

2 teaspoons balsamic vinegar

1 teaspoon dried oregano

Pinch of sugar

Pinch of salt

PIZZA DOUGH

| Dissolve the yeast in ½ cup plus 2 tablespoons (15 cl) warm water with the honey and olive oil.

| In a mixing bowl, mix the flour and salt, make a hollow in the middle and gradually stir in the yeast mixture with a wooden spoon.

| Knead the dough for about 10 minutes, either by hand on a lightly floured surface or using a mixer or bread machine, until it's smooth and no longer sticky. Cover with a damp dishtowel or similar cloth and let rise for about 1 hour in a moist, draft-free place.

TOMATO SAUCE

| In a mixing bowl, stir the tomato puree with the garlic, balsamic vinegar, oregano, sugar, and salt.

| Preheat the oven to 450°F (230°C).

| Depending on the style of pizza you choose, chop the ingredients for its toppings.

| Stretch the pizza dough into a circle and lay it on a perforated pizza pan or lightly oiled baking sheet. You could also line the baking sheet with parchment paper.

| Spread the sauce over the dough and drizzle with olive oil.

| Bake the pizza for 10 to 15 minutes or until the crust is lightly browned and the sauce is hot and bubbling.

MARGARITA PIZZA TOPPINGS

1 ball buffalo mozzarella

Fresh basil

4 SEASONS PIZZA TOPPINGS

4 ounces (100 grams) sliced white mushrooms

2 slices ham

4 marinated artichoke hearts

MARINARA PIZZA TOPPINGS

2 cloves garlic

Dried oregano and anything else you like (except canned pineapple!)

Olive oil

NOTE

EAT THE PIZZA RIGHT FROM THE OVEN. HOMEMADE PIZZA DOES NOT KEEP WELL.

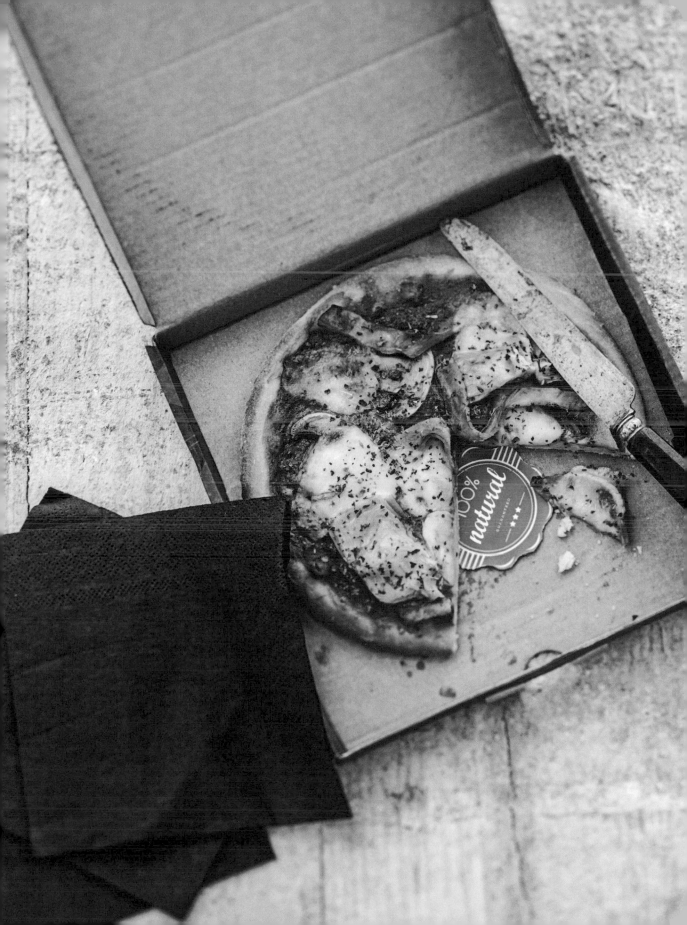

FAST FOOD *Moderate*

FISH STICKS

You may only have bought them frozen, so all the more reason to make your own. They will taste so much better.

❘ Put the fish in the freezer for 1 hour to make it easier to cut into pieces.

❘ Spread the flour in a shallow dish and mix it with salt and pepper. Put the egg white in another bowl and beat it lightly with a fork. Spread the breadcrumbs in a third dish.

❘ Using a sharp knife, cut the frozen fish into sticks about 3½ inches (9 cm) long and 1 inch (2.5 cm) wide.

❘ Coat the fish sticks first in the flour, then in the egg white, and finally in the breadcrumbs.

❘ Pour the oil into a skillet and fry the fish sticks for 5 minutes on each side over high heat until they're golden and cooked through.

❘ Drain the fish sticks on paper towels and serve them hot with tartar sauce or Béarnaise (see page 77).

HOMEMADE BREADCRUMBS

❘ Preheat the oven to 200°F (93°C).

❘ Cut the bread into pieces and lay them on a baking sheet. Bake for about 30 minutes until crispy and dry.

❘ Turn the bread into crumbs in a blender or food processor.

MAKES:
8 SERVINGS

PREPARATION
about 15 minutes

FREEZING
1 hour

COOKING
about 10 minutes

INGREDIENTS
14 ounces (400 grams) thick mild white fish fillets, such as cod, halibut, or haddock

⅓ cup (50 grams) all-purpose flour

2 pinches salt

Freshly ground white pepper

1 large egg white

2 cups (120 grams) Homemade Breadcrumbs (see below)

4 teaspoons oil, for cooking

MAKES:
ABOUT 2 CUPS (120 GRAMS)

PREPARATION
about 5 minutes

COOKING
about 30 minutes

INGREDIENTS
4 slices stale bread (120 grams)

BURRITOS

Less expensive than a flight to Cancún and a lot less hassle, burritos are easy to make—and you can fill them with anything you want.

**MAKES:
6 SERVINGS**

PREPARATION
about 1 hour

STANDING TIME
about 40 minutes

COOKING
10 to 12 minutes

INGREDIENTS
½ cup plus
2 tablespoons (15 cl)
milk

2 cups (250 grams)
all-purpose flour (plus a
little for rolling)

2 teaspoons Homemade
Chemical Leavener
(page 40)

2 teaspoons sugar

¼ teaspoon salt

2 teaspoons sunflower
or canola oil

TORTILLAS

| Warm the milk in a pan.

| In a bowl, mix the flour, leavener, sugar, and salt. Make a hollow in the middle and add the warm milk and the oil. Mix well and knead the dough for 2 to 3 minutes. Alternatively, use a mixer or bread machine. Wrap the dough in plastic wrap and let it rest for 30 minutes at room temperature.

| Divide the dough into 6 or 8 pieces (according to the size of your pan). Roll them by hand into balls and let the balls rest at room temperature for 10 minutes longer.

| Flatten each ball into a thin circle about 8 inches (20 cm) in diameter, regularly turning it and dusting it with flour so that it doesn't stick.

| Heat a heavy skillet (preferably cast-iron) or a large, flat griddle and cook each tortilla for about 45 seconds on each side. The tortillas should be soft enough to roll. The tortillas will keep for up to 48 hours in a sealed plastic bag.

NOTE

TORTILLAS FREEZE WELL PROVIDED THEY ARE SEPARATED BY SHEETS OF WAX PAPER.

**MAKES:
6 SERVINGS**

PREPARATION
about 10 minutes

INGREDIENTS
2 ripe avocados

Juice of 1 lime

A few sprigs fresh cilantro

Salt and freshly ground
pepper

½ onion, thinly sliced

GUACAMOLE

| Cut the avocados in half and remove the pits. Peel and chop the avocados.

| Transfer the avocado to a blender or food processor. Add the lime juice and cilantro and season with salt and pepper. Mix until creamy.

| Turn the avocado into a bowl and gently stir in the onion slices. The guacamole will keep if covered for up to 24 hours in the refrigerator.

NOTE

GUACAMOLE IS BEST IF EATEN IMMEDIATELY, ALTHOUGH IT WILL KEEP FOR A DAY.

MAKES:
6 SERVINGS

PREPARATION
about 1 hour

COOKING
about 20 minutes

INGREDIENTS
1 green or red bell pepper

1 onion

2 teaspoons sunflower or canola oil

1 pound (500 grams) ground sirloin steak

1 14- or 15-ounce (400 grams) can strained tomatoes or tomato puree

½ teaspoon cumin

½ teaspoon paprika

½ teaspoon ground coriander

Pinch of sugar

Salt and freshly ground pepper

1 14- or 15-ounce (400 grams) can red beans, drained

INGREDIENTS
6 tortillas (page 66)

Guacamole (page 66)

GARNISHES
Sour cream

Grated cheddar cheese

Diced tomatoes

Diced bell peppers

Chopped lettuce

Cooked rice

STEAK FILLING

| Finely chop the pepper and onion.

| Heat the oil in a skillet and when hot, cook the pepper and onion over medium-high heat for about 1 minute to soften. Add the ground beef and cook for about 5 minutes, stirring regularly, until the meat browns.

| Add the tomatoes, the spices, and the sugar. Season with salt and pepper, cover, and let simmer for about 10 minutes.

| Add the beans to the skillet and continue cooking for about 5 minutes until heated through. Keep on low heat until ready to serve.

| The filling will keep for up to 48 hours in the refrigerator and 2 months in the freezer.

PUTTING IT ALL TOGETHER

| Microwave the tortillas for 10 to 20 seconds just to warm them up.

| Fill each one with a little guacamole and a few spoonfuls of the steak mixture. Top with any combination of the garnishes.

TARTE FLAMBÉE

A specialty of Alsace in eastern France, Tarte Flambée is a little like pizza, and just as easy to make. Why not try it for a change?

**MAKES:
1 LARGE TART**

PREPARATION
about 20 minutes

STANDING TIME
10 minutes

COOKING
about 10 minutes

INGREDIENTS
4 teaspoons canola oil

2 cups (250 grams)
all-purpose flour

½ teaspoon salt

7 tablespoons (10 cl)
heavy cream

8 ounces (225 grams)
cream cheese

Freshly ground pepper

Grated nutmeg

¾ cup (200 grams)
cubed bacon (about
7 grams)

2 large onions, finely
sliced

| Preheat the oven to 450°F (230°C).

| Mix the oil with ¾ cup plus 2 tablespoons (20 cl) of warm water.

| In a mixing bowl, mix the flour and salt. Make a hollow and add the oil and water.

| Stir and knead the dough for about 5 minutes until it holds together in a ball. Alternatively, use a bread machine or an electric mixer with a bread hook. Cover with plastic or a dishcloth while you prepare the topping.

| In a mixing bowl, stir together the cream and cream cheese until smooth. Season with pepper and nutmeg.

| Roll the dough on a lightly floured surface into a thin rectangle the size of a baking sheet. Lay the dough over the baking sheet (or roll the dough directly on the sheet). Spread the cream cheese over it, leaving a ⅜-inch (1-cm) gap around the edges. Cover with the bacon and sliced onion.

| Bake for about 10 minutes as close to the bottom of the oven as possible until the edges of the tart are browned and slightly blistered and the bacon is cooked. Serve immediately.

VARIATION
SPRINKLE THE TART WITH GRATED SWISS CHEESE, SLICES OF STRONGER-TASTING CHEESE, OR SLICED MUSHROOMS.

NOTE
TARTE FLAMBÉE MUST BE EATEN STRAIGHT FROM THE OVEN!

QUICHE PASTRY

You don't have to be a pastry chef to make pastry for quiches and tarts. When you discover how simple it is, you'll never buy frozen quiches again.

TRADITIONAL PASTRY

| Mix the flour and salt in a bowl. Make a hollow in the middle and add the cubes of butter and then work the mixture with your fingers until coarsely crumbled.

| Add 2 to 4 teaspoons of cold water, 1 at a time, until the pastry forms a ball. Wrap it in plastic wrap and refrigerate for 30 minutes. The wrapped ball of pastry will keep in the refrigerator for 3 days and in the freezer for 2 months.

| When ready to use, roll the pastry into a thin circle on a lightly floured surface or between 2 silicone mats.

CHEESE PASTRY

| Mix the flour and salt in a bowl. Make a hollow in the middle and add the cheese and then lightly knead the pastry. Add the cubes of butter and mix for 2 to 3 minutes longer, until the pastry forms a ball. Wrap it in plastic wrap and refrigerate for 30 minutes. The wrapped ball of pastry will keep in the refrigerator for 3 days and in the freezer for 2 months.

| When ready to use, roll the pastry into a thin circle on a lightly floured surface or between 2 silicone mats.

MAKES:
4 TO 6 SERVINGS

PREPARATION
about 1 hour

REFRIGERATION
30 minutes

INGREDIENTS
2 cups (250 grams) all-purpose flour (plus a little for rolling)

2 pinches salt

½ cup (125 grams) cold butter, cut into cubes

MAKES:
4 TO 6 SERVINGS

PREPARATION
1 hour

REFRIGERATION
30 minutes

INGREDIENTS
1¾ cups (200 grams) all-purpose flour

Pinch of salt

1.5 ounces (50 grams) Petit-Suisse (see page 32) or Swiss cheese, cut into pieces

7 tablespoons (90 grams) soft butter, cut into cubes

QUICHE LORRAINE

| Preheat the oven to 350°F (180°C).

| Roll the pastry into a thin 12- to 13-inch (30- to 35-cm) circle and transfer to a lightly buttered, 10-inch (25-cm) quiche pan. Push it gently into the pan.

| Prick the bottom of the pastry with a fork and cover with parchment paper and weight with uncooked rice, chickpeas, or lentils. Bake for about 10 minutes. The pastry will only be partly baked. Take it from the oven and set on a wire rack while you prepare the filling. Remove the parchment paper and weights.

| Beat the eggs with the cream. Season with nutmeg and plenty of pepper. Go easy on the salt, as the bacon is salty.

| Scatter the ham and bacon over the bottom of the pastry and then gently pour the beaten eggs and cream over them. Bake for about 30 minutes or until the quiche is set and the pastry is lightly browned.

VARIATIONS:
SALMON & SPINACH QUICHE

Melt a tablespoon of butter in a sauté pan over medium-high heat. Sauté 8 ounces (225 grams) of frozen chopped spinach (let it thaw first). Drain the spinach. Poach 2 salmon fillets for about 10 minutes or until cooked through. Pull the salmon into pieces and then use them and the spinach in the above recipe in place of the ham and bacon.

GOAT CHEESE & VEGETABLE QUICHE

Substitute 11 ounces (300 grams) of cooked ratatouille (leftover or store-bought) and a 7-ounce (200-gram) log of goat cheese, cut into slices, for the ham and bacon in the above recipe.

MAKES:
1 10-INCH QUICHE
(4 TO 6 SERVINGS)

PREPARATION
about 1 hour

COOKING
about 40 minutes

INGREDIENTS
1 recipe Traditional Pastry (see page 70)

3 large eggs, preferably free-range

1¼ cups (30 cl) light cream

Grated nutmeg

Salt and freshly ground pepper

5 ounces (150 grams) ham, diced

5 ounces (150 grams) cubed bacon

71

HOT DOGS

Hot dogs with homemade buns and mustard are enough to make your mouth water!

**MAKES:
6 BUNS**

PREPARATION
about 30 minutes

STANDING TIME
1 hour 30 minutes

COOKING
about 15 minutes

INGREDIENTS
1 packet active dry yeast (each packet weighs ¼ ounce)

½ cup plus 2 tablespoons (15 cl) warm skim milk

1 level teaspoon sugar or honey

4 cups (500 grams) unbleached flour (plus a little for rolling)

1 level teaspoon salt

2 large eggs, preferably free-range

1 tablespoon soft butter, cut into cubes

Sesame or poppy seeds

THE BUNS

| In a large bowl, dissolve the yeast in the warm milk. Stir well and then add the sugar or honey.

| In another large mixing bowl, mix the flour and salt. Make a hollow in the middle and pour in the yeast mixture. Add 1 whole egg and the yolk from the other (reserve the egg white for later use). Mix the dough until crumbly and then turn out onto a lightly floured surface and knead for 5 to 6 minutes. Add the butter cubes and knead for 5 to 6 minutes longer until the dough is soft and pliable. Cover with a damp dishcloth and let rise for 1 hour at room temperature.

| Punch the dough down to release the air. Divide the dough into 6 equal pieces (approximately 4 ounces (125 grams) each. Roll each piece on a lightly floured surface into 6 buns about 4 inches (10 cm) long and the shape of a hot dog bun.

| Put the buns on a baking tray lined with parchment paper or a silicone baking mat, cover with a damp dishcloth, and let rise for 30 minutes longer.

| Preheat the oven to 350°F (180°C).

| Brush the buns with the reserved egg white, sprinkle with sesame or poppy seeds, and bake for about 15 minutes, or until the buns are puffy and golden. The buns will keep, well wrapped, for about 24 hours.

MAKES:
6 SERVINGS

PREPARATION
about 5 minutes

COOKING
about 13 minutes

INGREDIENTS
6 pork, beef, or game
hot dogs

6 Buns (see page 72)

Mustard

Fried onions

Sauerkraut

MAKES:
ABOUT ½ CUP
(210 GRAMS)

PREPARATION
about 10 minutes

STANDING TIME
24 to 48 hours

INGREDIENTS
⅓ cup (75 grams)
yellow mustard seeds

5½ tablespoons (8 cl)
cider vinegar

2 teaspoons grapeseed
oil

1 teaspoon honey, such
as acacia or mixed
flower

1 teaspoon powdered
turmeric

1 teaspoon flour or
potato flour

1 level teaspoon salt

Pinch of powdered
ginger

THE DOGS

| Drop the hot dogs in boiling water and poach for about 10 minutes or heated through. Drain.

| In a preheated 350°F (180°C) oven, warm the buns for about 3 minutes. Slice them in half lengthwise and put a hot dog on the lower half. Garnish with some mustard, fried onions, sauerkraut, or other vegetables and top with the other half of the bun.

THE MUSTARD

| The day before making the mustard, rinse the mustard seeds in a fine-mesh sieve. Transfer to a small bowl with the vinegar. Add 7 tablespoons (10 cl) of water, stir gently, and let the seeds soak overnight.

| Pour the mixture into a mixer, blender or food processor. Add the honey, turmeric, flour, salt and ginger and mix for several minutes until it becomes a smooth paste. If you need to thin the paste, add 2 to 4 teaspoons of water. Mind your eyes when you remove the lid of the blender or food processor. Fresh mustard can make you cry!

| Pour the mustard into a pot and refrigerate without covering tightly for up to 2 days, so it will gradually lose its acidity.

| Two days later, tightly seal the pot. The mustard will continue to "soften" in the pot, but if you like it strong, you can eat it now. It will keep for 2 months in the refrigerator.

NOTE

WHEN STORING THE MUSTARD
IN THE REFRIGERATOR, COAT
THE SURFACE WITH OLIVE
OIL TO PREVENT IT FROM
DRYING OUT.

73

MAYONNAISE

MAKES:
ABOUT 1 CUP (225 G)

PREPARATION
about 15 minutes

COOKING
about 8 minutes

STANDING TIME
5 to 6 minutes

INGREDIENTS
2 large eggs, preferably free-range and as fresh as possible

1 teaspoon prepared mustard (see page 73)

¼ teaspoon salt

Few drops vinegar or lemon juice

¾ cup plus 2 tablespoons (20 cl) sunflower, grapeseed, or canola oil, or whatever oil you prefer, or a mixture of oils

Freshly ground pepper

Ever tried making mayonnaise and wound up with a runny mess? With this simple recipe, you can't go wrong!

| Boil 1 egg for 8 minutes in salted water. Drain and peel it under cool, running water.

| Remove the yolk from the egg and put it in a bowl. (Reserve the white for another use.) Let the yolk cool for about 5 minutes.

| Separate the remaining raw egg and reserve the white for another use. Add the raw yolk to the bowl with the cooked yolk. Add the mustard, salt, and 2 drops of vinegar or lemon juice. Mix well and let the mayonnaise sit for 1 minute.

| Gradually add the oil to the bowl little by little, mixing constantly. Each time you add a little oil, stir the mayonnaise until the oil is completely absorbed and the mayo is homogeneous before adding more.

| When all the oil has been absorbed, season with pepper. Then, if you wish, add more salt and vinegar or lemon juice to taste. Cover with plastic wrap and refrigerate for 24 hours.

NOTE

IF YOU INTEND TO REFRIGERATE THE MAYONNAISE, BE SURE TO MAKE IT WITH GRAPESEED OIL, WHICH WON'T HARDEN IN THE FRIDGE.

COCKTAIL SAUCE

MAKES:
1 CUP PLUS (275 G)

PREPARATION
about 5 minutes

INGREDIENTS
1 cup (225 g) Mayonnaise

2 tablespoons Homemade Ketchup (see page 55)

2 teaspoons brandy

2 drops Tabasco

Shrimp cocktail, avocado with cocktail sauce... Have yourself a '70s night with this simplest of recipes.

Mix all the ingredients . . . and that's it!

HOLLANDAISE SAUCE

Does it come from Holland or from Normandy? No one knows for certain, but it sure won't come out of a package this time!

MAKES:
ABOUT 1 CUP
(225 G)

PREPARATION
about 5 minutes

COOKING
10 to 15 minutes

INGREDIENTS
3 large egg yolks, preferably free-range

2 teaspoons white vinegar

10 tablespoons (150 grams) soft butter, cut into pieces

Juice of ½ lemon

Salt and freshly ground pepper

| In a heat-proof bowl, beat the egg yolks with the vinegar and 2 teaspoons of water. Set the bowl over hot water in a larger pan, taking care the bowl does not touch the water (you can use a double boiler).

| Cook the sauce over medium heat, whisking constantly until the sauce turns white, doubles in volume, and thickens (the whisk should leave marks in the sauce).

| Add the butter, piece by piece, mixing vigorously all the time, as if you were making mayonnaise. Be sure each piece of butter emulsifies before adding the next.

| Remove the hollandaise from the heat and stir in the lemon juice, salt, and pepper. Serve immediately; hollandaise does not keep well.

NOTE

HOLLANDAISE SAUCE IS LIKE MAYONNAISE BUT IS MADE OVER HEAT AND USES BUTTER RATHER THAN OIL. KEEP A CLOSE EYE ON IT AND IF IT LOOKS AS IF IT IS CURDLING, REMOVE IT FROM THE HEAT, ADD A COUPLE TEASPOONS OF WATER, AND STIR LIKE CRAZY.

BÉARNAISE SAUCE

**MAKES:
ABOUT ½ CUP
(100 G)**

PREPARATION
about 5 minutes

COOKING
10 to 15 minutes

INGREDIENTS
1 large shallot, finely chopped

10 fresh tarragon leaves, roughly chopped

2 teaspoons white wine

2 teaspoons wine vinegar

Salt and freshly ground pepper

3 large egg yolks, preferably free-range

½ cup plus 2 tablespoons (150 grams) soft butter, cut into pieces

4 teaspoons chopped fresh tarragon and chervil

| In a saucepan, mix the shallot with the fresh tarragon. Add the wine and vinegar and season with salt and pepper. Bring to a boil and cook, stirring, for a few minutes until the liquid nearly evaporates.

| Drain through fine-mesh sieve into a heat-resistant bowl and add the egg yolks, whisking to mix.

| Set the bowl over hot water in a larger pan, taking care the bowl does not touch the water (you can use a double boiler). Whisk constantly until the mixture turns pale yellow, doubles in volume, and thickens (the whisk should leave marks in the sauce).

| Add the butter, piece by piece, mixing vigorously all the time, as if you were making mayonnaise. Be sure each piece of butter emulsifies before adding the next.

| Remove from the heat, stir in the tarragon and chervil, and season to taste with salt and pepper, if needed. Serve immediately; the sauce does not keep.

NOTE

FOR A DELICIOUS VARIATION, ADD SOME FRESH MINT. THIS TURNS THE BÉARNAISE INTO PALOISE SAUCE (NAMED AFTER THE TOWN OF PAU IN SOUTHWESTERN FRANCE).

HOMEMADE
BARBECUE SAUCE

Whether it's for coating ribs, slopping on a burger, or dipping fries or nuggets in, your very own BBQ sauce is finger-lickin' good.

| In a large skillet, heat the oil over medium heat. Add the onion and garlic and cook gently until they soften. Add the brown sugar, stir well, and cook for about 1 minute until the sugar caramelizes.

| Add the tomato puree, wine, apple juice, Worcestershire sauce, vinegar, mustard, thyme, cumin, and cayenne. Season with salt and pepper. Bring to a boil, reduce the heat and simmer for about 40 minutes until the sauce thickens slightly.

| While it's still hot, pour the sauce into sterilized bottles or jars (for more on sterilizing, see page 140). The sauce will keep for 10 days in an unsterilized bottle or similar container in the refrigerator. It can be frozen for 3 months.

NOTE

FREEZE THE SAUCE IN AN
ICE TRAY SO THAT YOU CAN
DEFROST THE AMOUNT
YOU NEED WHEN
YOU NEED IT.

BUTTER COOKIES

MAKES:
ABOUT 30 COOKIES

PREPARATION
about 15 minutes

REFRIGERATION
30 minutes

COOKING
about 15 minutes

INGREDIENTS
1¾ cups (200 grams) all-purpose flour (plus a little for rolling)

¼ cup (50 grams) sugar

½ teaspoon Homemade Leavener (see page 40) or baking powder

¼ teaspoon salt

6 tablespoons (75 grams) butter, cut into pieces

¼ cup (50 grams) sour cream

½ teaspoon pure vanilla extract

These little cookies are nearly square and just about melt in your mouth, thanks to the sour cream. There is one difficulty: finding the right size cookie cutter.

| In a large mixing bowl, stir together the flour, sugar, leavener, and salt. Add the pieces of butter and using your fingers, work the dough until it's crumbly.

| Add the sour cream and vanilla extract and work the dough until it holds together in a ball. This can be done with an electric mixer or your hands. Wrap in plastic wrap and refrigerate for 30 minutes.

| Preheat the oven to 350°F (180°C).

| On a lightly floured work surface, roll the pastry into a very thin rectangle. Cut the rolled dough into nearly square rectangles measuring 2½ by 2 inches (6 by 5 cm). If you have a cookie cutter that is the right size, you can use it. Carefully transfer the rectangles to a baking sheet lined with parchment paper.

| Prick the cookies in several places with a fork and bake for about 15 minutes or until they darken to a pleasing cookie color. Remove the cookies from the baking sheet and let them cool on wire racks. These will keep in an airtight tin for about 10 days.

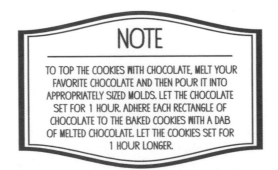

NOTE

TO TOP THE COOKIES WITH CHOCOLATE, MELT YOUR FAVORITE CHOCOLATE AND THEN POUR IT INTO APPROPRIATELY SIZED MOLDS. LET THE CHOCOLATE SET FOR 1 HOUR. ADHERE EACH RECTANGLE OF CHOCOLATE TO THE BAKED COOKIES WITH A DAB OF MELTED CHOCOLATE. LET THE COOKIES SET FOR 1 HOUR LONGER.

CINNAMON **COOKIES**

MAKES:
ABOUT 20 COOKIES

PREPARATION
about 15 minutes

REFRIGERATION
2 hours

COOKING
15 to 20 minutes

INGREDIENTS
⅓ cup (75 grams)
granulated sugar

¼ (50 grams)
Demerara or granulated
raw sugar

½ cup (100 grams) soft
butter

¾ cup plus 1 tablespoon
(125 grams) all-purpose
flour

3 tablespoons soy flour

2 tablespoons honey,
such as acacia or
mixed flower

1 teaspoon cinnamon

¼ teaspoon Homemade
Leavener (see page 40)
or baking powder

2 pinches salt

Originating from Belgium and Holland, where they are called speculaas, these small cookies are dark and crunchy.

| In a large bowl, work the white and Demerara sugars into the butter until creamy (this could be done in an electric mixer). Add both flours, the honey, cinnamon, leavener, and salt and stir until the mixture holds together in a ball. Wrap in plastic wrap and refrigerate for 2 hours.

| Preheat the oven to 325°F (170°C).

| Roll the dough between 2 sheets of wax paper or silicone mats until it's very thin. Cut into rectangles measuring about 2 by 1 inches (2.5 by 2 cm) using a sharp knife, or use an appropriately sized cookie cutter.

| Transfer the cookies to a baking sheet lined with parchment paper and leave ample space between each one (you may need 2 baking sheets), as they will expand in the oven. Bake for 15 to 20 minutes or until dark golden brown. Remove the cookies from the baking sheet and let them cool and harden on wire racks for at least 1 hour. The cookies will keep in an airtight tin for about 10 days.

NOTE

SOY FLOUR IS SOLD IN
HEALTH FOOD STORES AND SOME
SUPERMARKETS. IT'S YELLOWER
THAN WHEAT FLOUR AND GIVES
THE COOKIES A NUTTY FLAVOR,
AS WELL AS A MORE
ATTRACTIVE COLOR.

CINNAMON **SPREAD**

How could you resist such a delicacy? In fact, why should you?

MAKES:
ABOUT ¾ CUP

PREPARATION
about 10 minutes

INGREDIENTS
7 ounces (200 grams) or about ¾ of a batch of Cinnamon Cookies (see page 82)

10 tablespoons (15 cl) condensed milk

2 teaspoons honey, such as acacia or mixed flower

¼ teaspoon cinnamon

Pinch of salt

| Put the cookies in a blender or food processor and reduce them to crumbs.

| Add the condensed milk, honey, cinnamon, and salt, and continue mixing to a paste. If the spread is too thick, add a little more milk.

| Spoon the spread into a sterilized glass jar (see page 140), seal, and refrigerate. The spread will keep for up to 10 days in a tightly lidded jar. Spread on fresh bread.

NOTE
AS WELL AS PUTTING THE SPREAD ON BREAD OR TOAST, USE IT AS A GLAZE FOR CAKES AND FOR CAKE DECORATION. IT ALSO GIVES A DISTINCTIVE FLAVOR TO TIRAMISU.

RICH **CHOCOLATE** COOKIES

PREPARATION
about 15 minutes

REFRIGERATION
30 minutes

COOKING
15 to 17 minutes

STANDING TIME
10 minutes

INGREDIENTS
4 ounces (125 grams) bittersweet or semisweet chocolate, coarsely chopped

1 cup (150 grams) all-purpose flour

2 tablespoons unsweetened cocoa powder

1 teaspoon baking soda

2 pinches salt

½ cup (125 grams) soft butter

¾ cup (125 grams) light brown

1 large egg, preferably free-range

1 teaspoon pure vanilla extract

¾ cup (175 grams) semisweet chocolate chips

Cookies so chocolaty, you'll be tempted to do as the French do—dunk them in a glass of milk!

| Melt the chocolate in the top of a double boiler.

| Sift the flour, cocoa, baking soda, and salt into a bowl.

| In another bowl, beat the butter and sugar until light and creamy. Add the melted chocolate, egg, and vanilla extract and stir. Add the flour mixture and mix well. Stir in the chocolate chips and refrigerate for at least 30 minutes so that the mixture thickens.

| Preheat the oven to 325°F (170°C).

| Put small balls of dough on a baking sheet lined with parchment paper or a silicone mat and bake for 10 to 12 minutes, depending on how crunchy you like your cookies.

| Let the cookies cool on the baking sheet for about 10 minutes and then transfer to a wire rack to cool. Hide the cookies well so that they don't all disappear! The cookies will keep for 3 or 4 days in an airtight tin.

USE AN ICE CREAM SCOOP TO MOLD BALLS OF DOUGH TO THE RIGHT SIZE AND SHAPE FOR THE COOKIES. MAKE SURE TO LEAVE PLENTY OF SPACE BETWEEN THE COOKIES, AS THEY EXPAND IN THE OVEN.

★★★ TIP ★★★

CREAM-FILLED COOKIES

Round or square, these luscious cream-filled cookies are as quintessentially French as the cancan.

MAKES:
12 COOKIES

PREPARATION
about 25 minutes

REFRIGERATION
2 hours

COOKING
20 to 25 minutes

STANDING TIME
1 hour

COOKIES

1¾ cups (200 grams) all-purpose flour

⅓ cup (75 grams) sugar

2 tablespoons rye flour

1 tablespoon whole-wheat flour

1 pinch salt

1 pinch Homemade Leavener (see page 40) or baking powder

½ cup (125 grams) soft butter, cut into pieces

¼ cup (50 grams) heavy cream

1 large egg yolk, lightly beaten

CHOCOLATE FILLING

1½ ounces (40 grams) bittersweet or semisweet chocolate

1½ ounces (40 grams) milk chocolate

1 teaspoon honey

2 tablespoons butter

1 teaspoon cocoa powder

VANILLA FILLING

⅔ cup (100 grams) confectioners' sugar

2 tablespoons butter

2 teaspoons milk

1 teaspoon pure vanilla extract

COOKIES

| Mix the all-purpose flour, sugar, rye and whole-wheat flours, salt, and leavener in a bowl. Add the butter and work into a coarse crumble with your fingers.

| Add the cream and knead vigorously to form a ball. Wrap the dough in plastic wrap and refrigerate for 2 hours.

| Heat the oven to 325°F (170°C).

| Roll the dough between 2 sheets of wax paper or silicone mats until very thin. Using a cookie cutter, cut out 24 circles that are 3 inches (7 cm) in diameter.

| Lay the cookies on a baking sheet lined with parchment paper or a silicone mat. Prick the cookies with a fork and then brush with the beaten egg yolk. Bake for about 20 minutes and then let the cookies cool on wire racks.

CHOCOLATE FILLING:

| Melt the bittersweet and milk chocolate and the honey in the top of a double boiler. Remove from the heat and mix in the butter and cocoa powder.

| Put a teaspoonful of the mixture in the center of a cookie. Press another cookie on top of the chocolate until the filling reaches the edges of the sandwich cookie. Repeat to make 12 cookies. Let the cookies set at room temperature for 1 hour to give the filling time to harden.

VANILLA FILLING

| Beat together the confectioners' sugar, butter, milk, and vanilla to make a paste. Fill the cookies with the vanilla filling as you do with the chocolate filling.

| The filled cookies will keep for up to 1 week in an airtight tin.

CHOCOLATE-COVERED STRAWS

MAKES:
ABOUT 30 STRAWS

PREPARATION
about 20 minutes

REFRIGERATION
30 minutes

FREEZING
15 minutes

COOKING
about 20 minutes

INGREDIENTS
1 cup (150 grams) all-purpose flour (plus a little for rolling)

¼ cup (50 grams) sugar

¼ teaspoon Homemade Leavener (see page 40) or baking powder

2 pinches salt

¼ cup (50 grams) butter, cut into pieces

3 to 4 teaspoons (4 to 5 cl) cold milk

5 ounces (150 grams) bittersweet, semisweet, milk, or white chocolate (according to taste)

You can't drink through them, but your cup of coffee will taste so much better accompanied by these straws.

| In a bowl, mix together the flour, sugar, leavener, and salt. Add the butter and work into a crumble with your fingers.

| Add the milk little by little until the dough forms a ball; use your hands or a mixer. Wrap the dough in plastic wrap and refrigerate for 30 minutes.

| Roll the dough between 2 sheets of wax paper or silicone mats and transfer to a baking sheet. Freeze for 15 minutes.

| Preheat the oven to 350°F (180°C).

| Using a sharp knife, cut the dough into very narrow strips measuring about 4 inches long (10 cm). Roll them gently on a floured board or work surface until they're cylindrical and about 5 inches long (about 13 cm).

| Put the straws on a baking sheet lined with parchment paper and bake for about 15 minutes, until the ends are golden. Let the straws cool on a wire rack.

| Melt the chocolate in the top of a double boiler. Dip the straws in the melted chocolate, leaving about 1 inch (2.5 cm) at one end uncoated.

| Put them on wire racks until the chocolate hardens. The straws keep for up to 3 days in an airtight tin.

NOTE

FOR "INSTANT" CHOCOLATE STRAWS, DIP BREAD STICKS IN MELTED CHOCOLATE. JOB DONE!

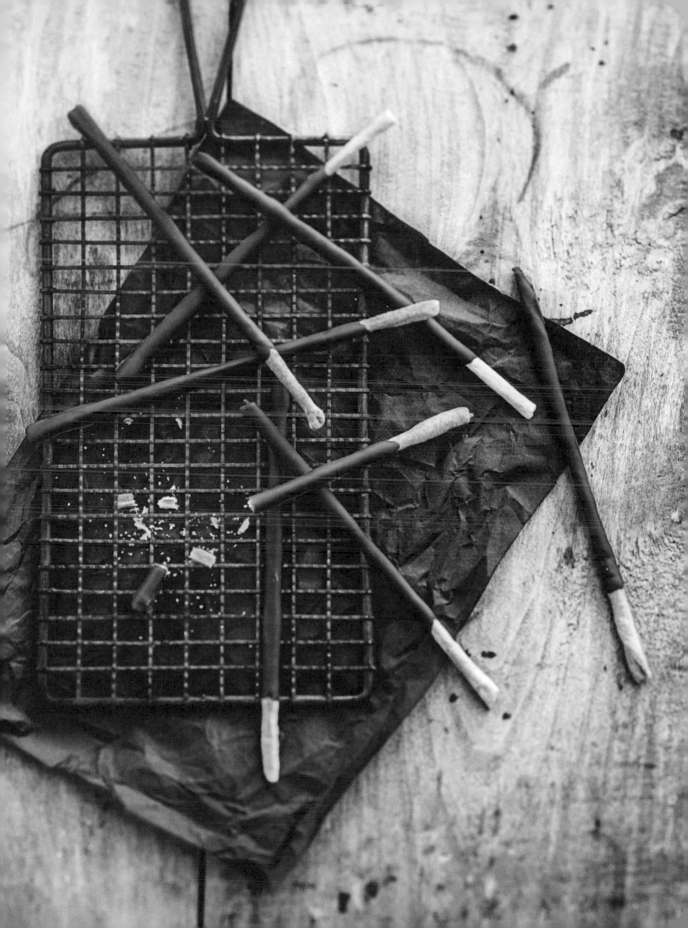

ORANGE CHOCOLATE COOKIES

**MAKES:
ABOUT 20 COOKIES**

PREPARATION
about 40 minutes

REFRIGERATION
1 hour

COOKING
about 20 minutes

FREEZING
20 minutes

INGREDIENTS
¾ cup (170 grams)
orange marmalade

Pinch of agar powder

3 large eggs, preferably
free-range

Pinch of salt

6 tablespoons
(75 grams) sugar

½ cup (75 grams)
all-purpose flour

1 teaspoon sunflower or
canola oil

7 ounces (200 grams)
bittersweet or semisweet
chocolate

Take a soft cookie, cover it with marmalade and coat it with crispy chocolate: A recipe for happiness!

| In a saucepan, mix the marmalade with 4 teaspoons (5 cl) of water, bring to a boil, sprinkle with the agar, and mix vigorously. Let the marmalade simmer for 2 minutes.

| Put a teaspoonful of the marmalade into each cup of a 20-cup mini muffin pan and let the marmalade cool to room temperature. When cool, refrigerate for 1 hour.

| Preheat the oven to 350°F (180°C).

| Separate the eggs and, with an electric mixer, whisk the whites with the salt in a bowl until stiff.

| Sprinkle the sugar over the egg whites and whisk for another minute. Add the egg yolks, 1 at a time, whisking all the time, and then beat in the flour. Finally, add the oil and mix gently.

| Pour the batter onto a baking sheet lined with parchment paper. Spread it to an even thickness to cover the baking sheet. Bake for about 10 minutes and then let it cool on the baking sheet.

| With a cookie cutter, cut out circles about 2 inches (5 cm) in diameter, wasting as little as possible. Set the cutout circles on the same lined baking sheet and bake for about 5 minutes to dry the cookies.

| Spread each cookie with the refrigerated marmalade mixture and then put the cookies on a baking sheet and freeze for 1 hour.

| Melt the chocolate in the top of a double boiler.

| Remove the cookies from the freezer and, using a soft spatula, coat each one with a thin layer of melted chocolate. The difference in temperature between the marmalade and the chocolate will cause the chocolate to solidify almost instantly into a crisp layer.

| Transfer the cookies to a rack as soon as they're finished to let the chocolate harden completely before eating. The cookies keep for up to 5 days in an airtight tin.

CRUNCHY CHOCOLATE-COATED
COOKIES

**MAKES:
ABOUT 25 COOKIES**

PREPARATION
about 15 minutes

REFRIGERATION
30 minutes

COOKING
15 minutes

STANDING TIME
1 hour

INGREDIENTS
1 cup (90 grams) rolled
oats

1¾ cups (200 grams)
bread flour

⅓ cup (75 grams) sugar

1 tablespoon vanilla
sugar (see page 36)

1 teaspoon baking soda

2 pinches salt

10 tablespoons
(150 grams) butter, cut
into pieces

2 tablespoons milk

7 ounces (200 grams)
bittersweet, semisweet
or milk chocolate
(whichever you prefer)

There are two types of people: those who like their cookies coarse and crunchy and those who prefer them smooth and crumbly. There's no accounting for it; that's just the way it is!

| Preheat the oven to 350°F (180°C).

| In a bowl, stir the rolled oats for a few seconds and then add the flour, sugar, vanilla sugar, baking soda, and salt. Add the butter and mix into a crumble with your fingers.

| Add the milk and mix vigorously until the dough forms a ball. Wrap in plastic wrap and refrigerate for 30 minutes.

| Roll the dough between 2 silicone mats or sheets of parchment paper until very thin. With a cookie cutter, cut out circles about 2 inches (5 cm) in diameter.

| Put the cookies on a baking sheet lined with parchment paper and prick with a fork before baking for about 15 minutes. Cool on the baking sheet.

| Melt the chocolate in the top of a double boiler, then temper the chocolate (see page 140) if you want it really shiny. Dip the cookies one by one in the chocolate, smooth with your finger to remove any excess, and let harden for 1 hour at room temperature before eating. The cookies will keep for up to 1 week in an airtight tin.

GOOD TO KNOW
YOU CAN BUY BREAD FLOUR
FROM A HEALTH FOOD STORE.

CRUMBLY CHOCOLATE
COOKIES

MAKES:
ABOUT 20 COOKIES

PREPARATION
about 15 minutes

REFRIGERATION
1 hour

COOKING
about 25 minutes

STANDING TIME
2 hours

INGREDIENTS
¾ cup plus 1 tablespoon (125 grams) all-purpose flour

⅓ cup (20 grams) grated coconut

3 tablespoons sugar

½ teaspoon baking soda

Pinch of salt

6 tablespoons (75 grams) butter, cut into pieces

1 tablespoon honey, such as acacia or mixed flower

5 ounces (150 grams) bittersweet, semisweet or milk chocolate

Whether it wears a dark chocolate or milk chocolate hat, it's ready for a showdown with the crunchy chocolate cookies. Whose side are you on?

| In a bowl, mix the flour, coconut, sugar, baking soda, and salt. Hollow out the middle and add the butter, honey, and 1 tablespoon of water. Mix the dough for 1 minute and then wrap in plastic wrap and refrigerate 1 hour.

| Preheat the oven to 350°F (180°C).

| Roll the dough between 2 silicone mats or sheets of parchment paper until very thin. Using a cookie cutter, cut out circles about 2 inches (5 cm) in diameter.

| Put them on a baking sheet lined with parchment paper and bake for about 10 minutes, until they're uniformly golden brown. Cool the cookies on a wire rack.

| Melt your chosen chocolate in the top of a double boiler, then dip the cookies in the melted chocolate so that one side is coated. Make patterns in the chocolate with a fork.

| Put the cookies on a rack and leave for at least 2 hours at room temperature to let the chocolate harden before eating. The cookies will keep for up to 1 week in an airtight tin.

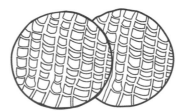

DINOSAUR COOKIES

**MAKES:
ABOUT 12 COOKIES**

PREPARATION
about 20 minutes

REFRIGERATION
30 minutes

COOKING
15 to 17 minutes

STANDING TIME
2 hours

INGREDIENTS
1 cup (175 grams) all-purpose flour (plus a little for rolling)

⅓ cup (50 grams) whole-wheat flour

⅓ cup (50 grams) rye flour

⅓ cup (75 grams) sugar

1 tablespoon vanilla sugar (see page 36)

½ teaspoon salt

½ teaspoon baking soda

½ cup (125 grams) butter, cut into pieces

1 large egg, preferably free-range

1 tablespoon milk

7 ounces (200 grams) bittersweet or semisweet chocolate, coarsely chopped

Chocolate cookies in the shape of a brontosaurus or diplodocus (depending on the cookie cutters you find) will be a big hit at a kids' party.

| In a bowl, mix the all-purpose, whole-wheat and rye flours with the sugar, vanilla sugar, salt, and baking soda. Add the butter and work into a crumble with your fingers. Add the egg and milk and knead into a ball. Wrap in plastic wrap and refrigerate for 30 minutes.

| Preheat the oven to 350°F (180°C).

| Roll the dough on a lightly floured board or work surface until it's very thin. Using cookie cutters, cut out the dinosaur shapes.

| Put them on a baking sheet lined with parchment paper or a silicone mat and bake for 10 to 12 minutes until the cookies are lightly browned. Cool the cookies on a wire rack.

| Melt the chocolate in the top of a double boiler and temper it (see page 140) to make it really shiny. Dip the cookies quickly in the melted chocolate, which should ideally coat them thickly. Create hollows and ridges as required with a fork. Let them set on wire racks for 2 hours at room temperature before eating. The cookies will keep for up to 1 week in an airtight tin.

NOTE

COAT THE DINOSAURS IN MILK CHOCOLATE IF YOUR LITTLE T-REXES PREFER. YOU DON'T HAVE TO TEMPER THE CHOCOLATE UNLESS YOU WANT IT VERY SHINY.

EMBUSCADES

An embuscade is an ambush, which is what lies in store for anyone who steals one of these innocent-looking cookies with a chocolate and hazelnut filling.

MAKES:
ABOUT 15 COOKIES

PREPARATION
about 15 minutes

REFRIGERATION
30 minutes

COOKING
about 10 minutes

INGREDIENTS
2 cups (250 grams) all-purpose flour (plus a little for rolling)

¼ cup (125 grams) sugar

1 teaspoon Homemade Leavener (see page 40) or baking powder

2 pinches salt

4 tablespoons (60 grams) butter, cut into pieces

1 large egg, preferably free-range

about 1 tablespoon milk (plus a little for coating)

Chocolate-Hazelnut Spread (see page 6)

| In a bowl, mix the flour, sugar, leavener, and salt. Add the butter and work into a crumble with your fingers. Add the egg and milk and knead into a ball (or use a mixer). Wrap in plastic wrap and refrigerate for 30 minutes.

| Preheat the oven to 350°F (180°C).

| Roll the dough on a lightly floured board or work surface or a silicone mat until very thin.

| Using a cookie cutter, cut out circles that are 1¾ to 2 inches (4.5 cm) in diameter.

| On half of the pastry circles, put a teaspoonful of Chocolate-Hazelnut Spread. Top each with another dough circle. Seal the filling by squeezing the edges together.

| Transfer the filled cookies to a baking sheet lined with parchment paper, brush them lightly with milk, and bake for about 10 minutes.

| Let the cookies cool on wire racks. The cookies will keep for up to 1 week in an airtight tin.

FIG ROLL COOKIES

MAKES:
ABOUT 30 COOKIES

PREPARATION
30 minutes

REFRIGERATION
30 minutes

COOKING
about 15 minutes

INGREDIENTS
7 ounces (200 grams)
soft, semi-dried figs

Pinch of cinnamon

2 cups (250 grams)
all-purpose flour

¼ cup (50 grams) sugar

Pinch of Homemade
Leavener (see page 40)
or baking powder

Pinch of salt

½ cup (125 grams)
butter, cut into pieces

Delicious cookies that give you an energy boost: What more could you ask for?

| Remove the stems from the figs and cut them into pieces. Put them in a bowl and sprinkle with cinnamon. Mix into a paste. If you're using a mixer, work in bursts so that the fig mixture doesn't overheat.

| Spoon the paste onto a large sheet of parchment paper, cover with another sheet of parchment and roll into a thin rectangle measuring about 10 by 5 inches (25 by 13 cm). Put the whole thing in the refrigerator to set while you make the cookie dough.

| In a bowl, mix the flour, sugar, leavener, and salt. Add the butter and work into a crumble with your fingers. Add about a tablespoon cold water and knead into a ball. Wrap in plastic wrap and refrigerate for 30 minutes.

| Preheat the oven to 350°F (180°C).

| Roll the dough between 2 sheets of parchment paper or silicone mats into a large square. Cut into strips about 2 inches (6 cm) wide.

| Spread a ⅜-inch-wide (1-cm) ribbon of fig mixture down the center of each strip of dough and fold over the sides, overlapping them slightly on top of the fig filling. Press firmly to seal.

| Slice part of the way through the strips every ⅜ inch (1 cm). Press the tines of a fork into the dough to flatten the cookies slightly and make a pattern.

| Put the cookies on a baking sheet lined with parchment paper and bake for about 15 minutes. Cool on wire racks before eating. The cookies will keep for up to 1 week in an airtight tin.

ORANGE **CAKES**

When the French bite into these cakes, they can't help returning to childhood. The cookies may not remind you of being a child, but they will make you happy nevertheless.

MAKES:
ABOUT 30 CAKES

PREPARATION
about 30 minutes

COOKING
about 15 minutes

INGREDIENTS
3 large eggs, preferably free-range

½ cup plus 1 teaspoon (130 grams) sugar

3 tablespoons honey, such as acacia or mixed flower

Grated zest of 1 orange, preferably organic

1 cup (150 grams) all-purpose flour

Pinch of Homemade Leavener (see page 40) or baking powder

Pinch of salt

3 tablespoons butter, melted

Oil, to grease the mold

1 8-ounce jar orange marmalade

⅔ cup (100 grams) confectioners' sugar

1 tablespoon freshly squeezed orange juice

| Preheat the oven to 350°F (180°C).

| In a bowl, mix the eggs, sugar, honey, and orange zest. Add the flour, leavener, and salt, then stir in the melted butter.

| Lightly grease silicone mini muffin pans (30 muffin cups) and fill each one three-quarters full. Bake for 10 minutes.

| Remove from the oven, turn out the cakes while still hot, and cool for 5 minutes on a wire rack.

| Raise the oven temperature to 400°F (200°C).

| Cut a piece out of the bottom of each cake in the shape of a cone. Spoon some marmalade in the hollow and plug with the cone shape.

| Mix the confectioners' sugar and orange juice in a bowl.

| Dip the cakes "head first" in the confectioners' sugar mixture, making sure there's plenty of it on each cake. Put the cakes on a baking sheet lined with parchment paper. Bake for 3 minutes. The coating should turn white.

| Cool on a wire rack before eating. The cakes will keep for up to 3 days in an airtight tin.

PALM COOKIES

There is nothing crunchier than these cookies—provided you eat them straight from the oven.

MAKES:
ABOUT 30 COOKIES

PREPARATION
about 15 minutes

FREEZING
30 minutes

COOKING
about 15 minutes

INGREDIENTS
3 tablespoons
granulated sugar

1 tablespoon
confectioners' sugar

2 teaspoons vanilla
sugar (see page 36)

1 sheet (250 grams)
frozen puff pastry,
thawed

Flour for rolling

| In a bowl, mix the granulated, confectioners', and vanilla sugars.

| On a lightly floured board or work surface, gently roll the puff pastry into a thin rectangle, taking care not to crush the layers together.

| Dust the surface with one-quarter of the sugar mixture and press gently so that it sticks to the pastry. Fold the long edges of the pastry so that they meet in the center. Sprinkle the folded edges with another quarter of the sugar mixture. Fold halfway into the center. Sprinkle with another quarter of the sugar and roll each side into the center. You should now have a long double roll of sugar-coated pastry in the shape of a palm frond.

| Wrap tightly in parchment paper and freeze for 30 minutes.

| Preheat the oven to 400°F (200°C).

| Remove the roll from the freezer and roll it in the rest of the sugar mixture, pressing firmly to make it stick.

| With a sharp knife, slice the roll into very thin slices and put them on a nonstick baking sheet.

| Press your thumb gently into the base of each "palm" to keep the layers together and bake for about 15 minutes, watching to check that the sugar doesn't burn.

| Remove from the oven and cool before eating. The cookies will keep for up to 3 days in an airtight tin.

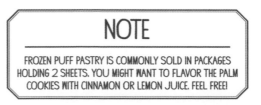

NOTE

FROZEN PUFF PASTRY IS COMMONLY SOLD IN PACKAGES HOLDING 2 SHEETS. YOU MIGHT WANT TO FLAVOR THE PALM COOKIES WITH CINNAMON OR LEMON JUICE. FEEL FREE!

CHOCOLATE-GLAZED FINGERS

MAKES: ABOUT 40 FINGERS

PREPARATION
30 minutes

REFRIGERATION
1 hour

COOKING
15 to 17 minutes

INGREDIENTS

½ cup (125 grams) soft butter

¼ cup (50 grams) sugar

½ teaspoon salt

Tiny pinch vanilla powder (see note)

1¾ cups (200 grams) all-purpose flour (plus a little for rolling)

Tiny pinch baking soda

9 ounces (250 grams) milk chocolate, coarsely chopped

Calling all milk chocolate lovers: These cookies are so good, you'll want to lick your fingers!

| In a bowl, whisk the butter, sugar, salt, and vanilla powder. Add the flour and baking soda and work the dough into a ball. Wrap in plastic wrap and refrigerate for 1 hour.

| Preheat the oven to 350°F (180°C).

| Break off pieces of dough the size of large hazelnuts and roll them on a lightly floured board or work surface into cylinders about 3 inches (7 cm) long and ⅜ inch (1 cm) in diameter.

| Put them on a baking sheet lined with parchment paper and bake for 10 to 12 minutes until lightly browned. Remove the fingers from the baking sheet and let them cool on wire racks.

| Melt the chocolate in the top of a double boiler. Dip the finger cookies in the melted chocolate and let them set on wire racks until the chocolate hardens. The chocolate fingers will keep for up to 1 week in an airtight tin.

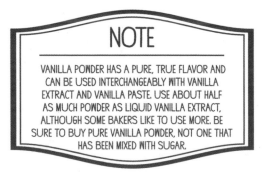

NOTE

VANILLA POWDER HAS A PURE, TRUE FLAVOR AND CAN BE USED INTERCHANGEABLY WITH VANILLA EXTRACT AND VANILLA PASTE. USE ABOUT HALF AS MUCH POWDER AS LIQUID VANILLA EXTRACT, ALTHOUGH SOME BAKERS LIKE TO USE MORE. BE SURE TO BUY PURE VANILLA POWDER, NOT ONE THAT HAS BEEN MIXED WITH SUGAR.

JAM BOATS

**MAKES:
ABOUT 20 BOATS**

PREPARATION
about 10 minutes

COOKING
about 15 minutes

INGREDIENTS
3 large eggs, preferably free-range

Pinch salt

⅓ cup (75 grams) sugar

½ cup (75 grams) all-purpose flour

Oil for greasing pan

Jam or whatever spread you like

The most difficult thing about this recipe is finding a muffin pan with molds that are the right shape. The rest is a piece of cake.

| Preheat the oven to 350°F (180°C).

| Separate the eggs and, using an electric mixer, whisk the whites with the salt until they're stiff. Sprinkle the sugar on top and whisk for 1 more minute. Add the egg yolks, 1 at a time, beating after each addition. Finally, beat in the flour.

| Lightly grease a silicone baking pan with boat-shaped molds. Spoon the batter into each one until it's four-fifths full. Bake for about 15 minutes until the surface is lightly browned.

| Remove from the oven, turn the little boats out onto a wire rack, and hollow out the center of each one with your finger or a knife handle.

| Let them cool a few minutes before filling the hollows with a teaspoonful of jam or spread. The cookies will keep for up to 3 days in an airtight tin.

NOTE

YOU CAN USE ALMOST ANY MINI MUFFIN PAN; THE SHAPE WON'T BE THE SAME, BUT THE FLAVOR WILL BE.

BRETON **BUTTER** COOKIES

Crunchy-crumbly and oozing butter, these cookies may originally be from Brittany, but they lack nothing in sophistication.

**MAKES:
ABOUT 20 COOKIES**

PREPARATION
about 15 minutes

REFRIGERATION
2 hours

COOKING
20 to 25 minutes

INGREDIENTS
½ cup plus
2 tablespoons
(150 grams) soft butter

½ cup (125 grams)
sugar

3 pinches salt

2 cups (250 grams)
all-purpose flour

1 tablespoon
Homemade Leavener
(see page 40) or baking
powder

3 large egg yolks,
preferably free-range

| Whisk the butter with the sugar and salt, using an electric mixer. Gradually sift in the flour and leavener. Add 2 of the egg yolks and knead into a ball as quickly as possible. Wrap in plastic wrap and refrigerate for 2 hours until firm.

| Preheat the oven to 350°F (180°C).

| Roll the dough between 2 sheets of silicone or parchment paper until it's ⅜ inch (1 cm) thick. Cut out circles about 2 inches (5.5 cm) in diameter and lay them flat in the bottom of the molds of ungreased, nonstick muffin pans. You will need enough muffin pans for 20 cookies.

| Beat the remaining egg yolk with a little water and brush it over the pastry circles. Bake for 20 to 25 minutes or until golden brown.

| Remove from the oven, then let cool a little in the muffin pan before turning out and cooling completely on wire racks. The cookies will keep for up to 10 days in an airtight tin.

NOTE

WORK QUICKLY WHEN MIXING THE DOUGH BECAUSE IF YOU KNEAD IT TOO LONG, THE COOKIES WILL LOSE THEIR LIGHTNESS.

ZEBRA **CAKE**

To jazz up a sponge cake with zebra stripes, all you have to do is alternate layers of vanilla batter with layers of chocolate batter—your oven will do the rest. The wonders of physics!

**MAKES:
1 LARGE CAKE;
8 SERVINGS**

PREPARATION
about 30 minutes

COOKING
about 50 minutes

STANDING TIME
15 minutes

INGREDIENTS
4 large eggs, preferably free-range

½ cup plus
3 tablespoons
(160 grams) sugar

2 cups (250 grams) all-purpose flour

½ cup (125 grams) butter, melted

¼ cup (6 cl) milk, plus 4 teaspoons for the cocoa mixture

1 tablespoon plus 2 teaspoons honey

2 teaspoons Homemade Leavener (see page 40) or baking powder

Pinch of salt

2 tablespoons cocoa powder

2 teaspoons pure vanilla extract

Oil for greasing pan

| Preheat the oven to 350°F (180°C). Weigh a large bowl (you'll find out why).

| Separate the eggs and beat the yolks with ½ cup (100 grams) of the sugar until the mixture lightens. Add the flour, melted butter, ¼ cup of milk, honey, leavener, and salt and mix well.

| Whisk the egg whites until they're stiff, sprinkling the remaining sugar on them at the last minute. Fold the meringue gently into the batter.

| Weigh the bowl with the mixture in it and subtract the weight of the empty bowl to give you the weight of the mixture. Remove exactly half the mixture and put in another bowl.

| Dissolve the cocoa powder in the remaining 4 teaspoons of milk. Blend the dissolved cocoa powder with half of the batter. Mix the vanilla extract into the other half.

| Pour a layer of the vanilla mixture into the bottom of a lightly greased springform pan. Spread a layer of the cocoa mixture on top of the vanilla layer. Continue alternating the mixtures until you have 5 layers, ending with a chocolate layer.

| Bake the cake for about 50 minutes. If the surface browns too quickly, cover it with parchment paper. To check whether the cake is cooked through, insert a knife blade into the center; it should come out "clean."

| Turn off the oven and prop the oven door halfway open. Let the cake cool for 15 minutes. Turn it out onto a wire rack to cool completely before slicing. The cake will keep for 3 days wrapped in foil in an airtight tin.

BROWNIES

They may be high in calories, but at least there's no high-fructose corn syrup or preservatives.

PREPARATION:
ABOUT 15 MINUTES

COOKING
about 35 minutes

REFRIGERATION
2 hours

INGREDIENTS

1⅓ cups (300 grams) bittersweet or semisweet chocolate, coarsely chopped

½ cup (125 grams) soft butter (plus a little for greasing the dish)

1 cup plus 2 tablespoons (150 grams) light brown sugar

1 teaspoon baking soda

Pinch of salt

3 large eggs, preferably free-range

3 tablespoons cornstarch

1 heaping tablespoon unsweetened cocoa powder

⅓ cup (75 grams) semisweet chocolate chips

| Preheat the oven to 350°F (180°C).

| Melt the chocolate and the butter in a large pan over low heat. Mix in the brown sugar, baking soda, and salt. Add the eggs, 1 at a time, mixing each in before adding the next.

| Add the cornstarch and cocoa powder and mix vigorously for 1 minute with a wooden spatula until the batter is smooth and shiny. Stir in the chocolate chips.

| Pour the batter into a buttered rectangular dish measuring about 12 by 8 inches (30 by 20 cm). Smooth the surface and bake for about 30 minutes until the batter is cooked through. To test, insert a knife blade into the center; when you pull it out, it should be "clean."

| Remove from the oven and let the brownies cool in the pan before refrigerating for 2 hours.

| Cut into squares before serving. The brownies will keep for 3 or 4 days in a tightly lidded plastic container in the refrigerator.

NOTE

IT'S IMPORTANT TO REFRIGERATE THE BROWNIES SO THAT THEY ARE PROPERLY FIRM. YOU CAN USE CHOPPED WALNUTS, ALMONDS, OR HAZELNUTS IN PLACE OF THE CHOCOLATE CHIPS IF YOU PREFER.

CARAMEL BARS

MAKES:
ABOUT 20 BARS

PREPARATION
about 1 hour

REFRIGERATION
1 hour

COOKING
about 40 minutes

FREEZING
1 hour

COOKIES

½ cup (125 grams) soft butter

¼ cup (50 grams) sugar

½ teaspoon salt

Tiny pinch of vanilla powder (see page 102)

1¾ cups (200 grams) all purpose flour

Pinch Homemade Leavener (see page 40) or baking powder

CARAMEL

1¾ cups (40 cl) sweetened condensed milk

¾ cup plus 2 tablespoons (20 cl) evaporated milk

2 teaspoons honey, such as acacia or mixed flower

1 tablespoon salted butter

COATING

4 ounces (125 grams) milk chocolate, coarsely chopped

4 ounces (125 grams) bittersweet or semisweet chocolate, coarsely chopped

An irresistible combination of butter cookie, caramel, and milk chocolate—try it at least once.

COOKIES

| In a bowl, beat the butter with the sugar, salt, and vanilla powder until creamy. Add the flour and leavener and mix until the dough forms a ball. Cover with a clean dishcloth and refrigerate for 1 hour.

| Preheat the oven to 300°F (150°C).

| Roll the dough until very thin, then cut it into strips measuring 4 inches long and ¾ inch wide (10 cm by 2 cm). Prick the strips, called bars, and put them on baking sheets lined with parchment paper or silicone mats. Bake for 20 minutes, then cool the bars on a wire rack.

CARAMEL

| In a deep pan, mix the sweetened condensed milk and the evaporated milk with the honey and gradually bring to a boil. Simmer for about 15 minutes, stirring continuously with a heat-resistant spatula and taking care not to let the mixture stiffen.

| Once the mixture has caramelized and turned a good, deep brown, remove the pan from the heat and mix in the butter until it melts.

| Spread 2 teaspoons of the caramel onto each baked bar and freeze for 1 hour.

COATING

| Melt the milk and bittersweet chocolates in the top of a double boiler. Using 2 forks to hold them, dip the bars in the melted chocolate. Put them on a wire rack until the coating sets. The caramel bars will keep for 3 days in an airtight tin.

COCONUT BARS

They're sooooo easy!

**MAKES:
ABOUT 20 BARS**

PREPARATION
about 15 minutes

STANDING TIME
1 hour

FREEZING
1 hour

COOKING
about 5 minutes

INGREDIENTS
1¾ cups (40 cl)
sweetened condensed
milk

2 cups (200 grams)
grated coconut

7 ounces (200 grams)
milk chocolate

| In a bowl, mix the milk and coconut. Cover with plastic wrap and let sit for about 1 hour at room temperature so the mixture can swell.

| Roll the sticky mixture between 2 sheets of parchment paper until it's about ⅜ inch thick (1 cm). Remove the top sheet and with a sharp knife, cut the mixture into rectangles measuring about 2½ inches by ¾ inch (6 by 2 cm). Put the rectangles on a baking sheet or tray lined with parchment paper. Freeze for at least 1 hour.

| Melt the chocolate in the top of a double boiler. Dip the frozen coconut rectangles into the melted chocolate. Set them on wire racks for the chocolate to harden. The coconut bars will keep for up to 3 days in an airtight tin.

PENGUIN COOKIES

These frosted and filled cookies are sure to make you smile.

**MAKES:
10 COOKIES**

PREPARATION
about 45 minutes

FREEZING
1 hour 30 minutes

COOKING
15 minutes

CHOCOLATE FOR THE CENTER

½ ounce bittersweet or semisweet chocolate, coarsely chopped

CREAM FILLING

2 sheets gelatin

4 teaspoons warm milk

1 cup plus 2 tablespoons (250 grams) mascarpone (9 ounces)

½ cup (12 cl) sweetened condensed milk

1 large egg white

COOKIE MIXTURE

3 large eggs, preferably free-range

¼ cup (60 grams) sugar

2 tablespoons butter, melted

3 tablespoons all-purpose flour

1 tablespoon cocoa powder

Pinch of salt

CHOCOLATE COATING

5 ounces (150 grams) bittersweet or semisweet chocolate

CHOCOLATE FOR THE CENTER

| Melt the chocolate in the top of a double boiler. Spread a sheet of silicone or parchment paper on a baking sheet and pour the melted chocolate on it. Spread it out as thinly as possible and then refrigerate until the chocolate has hardened again.

CREAM FILLING

| Soak the gelatin in a bowl of cold water for about 10 minutes. Drain and dilute the gelatin in the warm milk.

| Whisk the mascarpone and condensed milk together. Add the diluted gelatin and stir.

| Whisk the egg white until stiff, then gently fold it into the mascarpone mixture. Cover and refrigerate.

| Preheat the oven to 350°F (180°C).

COOKIE MIXTURE

| Separate the eggs and beat the yolks with the sugar. Mix in the melted butter.

| Sift the flour and cocoa powder over the batter, stirring to mix.

| Whisk the egg whites and salt until stiff. Gently fold the meringue into the batter.

| Pour the batter onto a silicone mat in a rimmed baking sheet. Spread the batter evenly over the sheet. Bake for 8 to 10 minutes.

| Turn the baked mixture out. Cut the rectangle in half and put each half on 2 equal-sized rectangles of parchment paper arranged on baking sheets.

| Spread half the cream filling in a thin layer on one of the rectangles and cover with the thin refrigerated sheet of chocolate. Pour the remainder of the cream filling over the chocolate and cover with the other rectangle. Be sure the rectangles are exactly aligned. Freeze for 1 hour 30 minutes.

| Remove the rectangle from the freezer, cut into smaller rectangles measuring about 3 by 1½ inches (8.5 by 3 cm) and put these right back in the freezer.

| Melt the remaining 5 ounces (150 grams) of chocolate in the top of a double boiler. Coat the cookies with thin layers of chocolate, using a silicone spatula. The chocolate will form a crust on contact with the ice-cold cookies.

| Put the penguins on a rack and refrigerate before eating. The cookies will keep for 3 days in the refrigerator.

CRUNCHY CHOCOLATE BARS

MAKES: 8 TO 9 BARS

PREPARATION
15 minutes

REFRIGERATION
1 to 2 hours

COOKING
about 5 minutes

INGREDIENTS
8 ounces (225 grams) milk chocolate, coarsely chopped

1 8½-ounce package (240 grams) sugar wafers, preferably chocolate-filled

Oil to grease the mold

Mini waffles coated with milk chocolate: Nothing too complicated here, but guaranteed after-school satisfaction.

| Melt the chocolate in the top of a double boiler.

| Lightly grease a large, rectangular silicone mold (or 2 silicone cake pans) and pour half the melted chocolate into it. Arrange the wafers side by side on the layer of chocolate and gently press on them. Pour the remaining chocolate over the wafers and smooth the surface. Refrigerate for 1 to 2 hours.

| Turn the chilled wafers out onto a work surface and break into separate bars.

| To make the bars look like those that are sold commercially, make 4 perpendicular grooves in the top of each bar with a knife. The bars will keep for up to 1 week in an airtight tin and refrigerated.

NOTE

NOW THAT YOU KNOW HOW TO MAKE CRUNCHY CHOCOLATE BARS, LET YOUR IMAGINATION RUN RIOT. EXPERIMENT WITH STRAWBERRY, VANILLA, OR PECAN FLAVORED WAFFLES. OR WHY NOT WHITE CHOCOLATE? HAVE FUN!

CARAMEL CANDIES

Little explosions of salty caramel wrapped in milk chocolate—seriously addictive. It's not easy to make them perfectly rectangular, but never mind. They taste just as good in any shape.

| In a deep nonstick pan, mix the sugar, butter, honey, and 2 teaspoons of water. Bring to a boil and cook over high heat until the mixture is light brown (it will register 300°F [150°C] on a candy thermometer).

| Add the almonds and mix them in quickly. Immediately pour the caramel onto a silicone mat in an ovenproof dish. Let cool a few moments.

| With a large knife, score the caramel into candy-size rectangles. This will enable you to break it up once it's hard. (If the caramel sticks to the knife or the marks disappear, you may have slightly overcooked the caramel, but it doesn't matter.) Let the caramel cool for 15 minutes or so longer, then snap along the marks to break it up.

| | Melt the chocolate in the top of a double boiler. Let it cool a little, then dip the caramel pieces into the melted chocolate. Put them on a wire rack and let the chocolate set for 1 hour at room temperature until the chocolate hardens before eating. The caramel will keep for 3 weeks in an airtight container.

**MAKES:
ABOUT 1½ POUNDS
(700 GRAMS)
CARAMELS**

PREPARATION
about 15 minutes

COOKING
about 10 minutes

STANDING TIME
1 hour

INGREDIENTS
½ cup plus
2 tablespoons
(150 grams) sugar

7 tablespoons
(90 grams) salted butter

2 tablespoons honey

1 tablespoon ground almonds

7 ounces (200 grams) milk chocolate

NOTE

IF YOU WIND UP WITH LUMPS OF CARAMEL STICKING TO THE SPATULA, DON'T WORRY. DIP THE SPATULA IN BOILING WATER AND LET THE CARAMEL MELT AWAY.

MARSHMALLOWS

MAKES: APPROXIMATELY 2 DOZEN

PREPARATION
about 20 minutes

COOKING
about 15 minutes

STANDING TIME
4 hours

INGREDIENTS
5 sheets of gelatin

3 large egg whites, preferably free-range

1 cup plus 2 tablespoons (250 grams) sugar

4 tablespoons (50 grams) honey, such as acacia or mixed flower

Seeds of 1 vanilla bean

⅓ cup (50 grams) confectioners' sugar

⅓ cup (50 grams) cornstarch

FLAVORED MARSHMALLOWS

2 teaspoons extract of your choice (rose, violet, mint, lemon)

¼ teaspoon food coloring (optional)

Whether you prefer them plain or flavored, one thing is for sure: With a mouthful of marshmallow, you will be at a loss for words!

| Soak the gelatin in cold water for about 10 minutes. Drain and dry thoroughly.

| In a large bowl, whisk the egg whites until stiff. Use a mixer on a medium setting.

| Pour ½ cup (12 cl) of water into a saucepan, add the sugar and honey. If making plain marshmallows, also add the vanilla seeds; if making another flavor of marshmallow, add the extract now instead of the vanilla bean seeds. Bring to a boil and cook until the syrup registers 225°F (100°C) on a candy thermometer.

| Pour the hot mixture slowly over the egg whites, whisking continuously. Add the gelatin while the marshmallow is still hot. Turn up the mixer's speed so that the marshmallow puffs up and turns shiny.

| If you want to add coloring, do so now. Continue mixing as the marshmallow cools. When it no longer feels hot to the touch (dip a finger in it from time to time), it's ready.

| Sift the confectioners' sugar and cornstarch into a bowl, then transfer the mixture to a shallow dish lined with parchment paper.

| Pour the marshmallow mixture on a nonstick baking sheet and spread it out with a soft spatula. Let cool for 4 hours at room temperature.

| Cut the marshmallow into whatever shape you like (strips, squares, etc.) then roll them in the confectioners' sugar mixture so that they don't stick together. Marshmallows keep for up to 10 days in an airtight container.

NOTE

IF YOU WANT YELLOW MARSHMALLOWS, THE BEST WAY TO COLOR THEM IS TO USE SAFFRON. ADD A PINCH OR TWO TO THE SUGAR SOLUTION BEFORE BRINGING IT TO A BOIL.

PRALINE

These are the peak of indulgence—chocolate and hazelnut merging with sweet praline.

MAKES:
ABOUT 10 PRALINES

PREPARATION
about 25 minutes

REFRIGERATION
1 hour

COOKING
about 10 minutes

PRALINE

5 ounces (150 grams) milk chocolate, coarsely chopped

5 ounces (150 grams) hazelnut praline paste

4 tablespoons (60 grams) butter, cut into pieces

1 tablespoon powdered milk

2 teaspoons cocoa powder, sifted

COATING

2 ounces (50 grams) whole hazelnuts

2 tablespoons sugar

5 ounces (150 grams) milk chocolate, coarsely chopped

| The praline: Melt the chocolate and the praline paste in the top of a double boiler. Remove from the heat and add the butter, powdered milk, and sifted cocoa powder.

| Pour the mixture into a silicone mold to a depth of 1 inch (2.5 cm) or so, cover with plastic wrap, and refrigerate for 1 hour to let it harden.

| Remove from the refrigerator and cut out circles about 1½ inches (3 cm) in diameter. Return these to the refrigerator while you make the coating.

| The coating: Chop up the hazelnuts and put them in a nonstick pan. Sprinkle with the sugar, cover, and cook over high heat until the sugar caramelizes.

| Melt the chocolate in the top of a double boiler and remove from the heat. Add the caramelized hazelnuts and stir to mix.

| Using a fork, dip the refrigerated circles of praline in the chocolate and hazelnut mixture, letting any excess fall off. Put them on a wire rack or baking sheet lined with parchment paper. Let them set for 20 minutes to give the chocolate time to harden. The pralines will keep for up to 5 days in an airtight container in the refrigerator.

NOTE

YOU CAN COAT THE PRALINES IN BITTERSWEET OR WHITE CHOCOLATE IF YOU PREFER. WHEN IT COMES TO INDULGENCE, ANYTHING GOES!

BUTTER CARAMELS

MAKES:
ABOUT 30
CARAMELS

PREPARATION
about 15 minutes

COOKING
about 20 minutes

STANDING TIME
overnight

INGREDIENTS
¾ cup plus 2 tablespoons (200 grams) sugar

½ cup (100 grams) honey, such as acacia or mixed flower

½ cup plus 2 tablespoons (15 cl) light cream

2 tablespoons salted butter, cut into pieces

Like many buttery treats, these candies are thought to have been invented in Brittany, but they are now enjoyed worldwide.

| Boil the sugar and honey over high heat until they caramelize (see page 24).

| Meanwhile, heat the cream until it registers about 175°F (80°C) on a candy thermometer. Do this on the stove or in the microwave.

| When the caramel is a pale golden color, remove it from the heat, and slowly pour the cream over it, mixing continuously with a wooden spatula. Be careful not to splash yourself, as it is very hot.

| Bring the mixture to a boil and cook until the caramel turns light brown (your thermometer should read 250°F (120°C). Remove from the heat, add the butter, a piece at a time, and mix until melted.

| Pour the caramel into a large, flat, rectangular dish lined with parchment paper. Smooth the surface while it's still hot and malleable. Leave overnight at room temperature to give the caramel time to harden.

| Cut into cubes with a serrated knife and wrap the cubes in plastic wrap—just like real candies. The caramels will keep for up to 3 weeks in an airtight container.

LOLLIPOPS

Perfect to make on a rainy Sunday afternoon!

MAKES:
10 LOLLIPOPS

PREPARATION
about 20 minutes

COOKING
about 20 minutes

STANDING TIME
1 hour

INGREDIENTS
½ cup (125 grams)
sugar

2 tablespoons honey,
such as acacia or
mixed flower

4 teaspoons your
favorite syrup or
natural flavoring

Liquid food coloring

| In a small saucepan, bring the sugar and 4 teaspoons of water to a boil. Add the honey and heat until the sugar melts and syrup reaches a temperature of 250°F (120°C) on a candy thermometer.

| Add the syrup or flavoring and the food coloring to make the syrup the color you want. Heat to 300°F (150°C) on a candy thermometer. As soon as this temperature is reached, plunge the pan in cold water to lower the temperature.

| Pour the mixture into small, round silicone molds and immediately insert lollipop sticks in the centers. Let the lollipops cool for 1 hour at room temperature. Pry the lollipops out of the molds...and suck!

| The lollipops will keep for 2 months if well wrapped in candy paper and kept in a dry place.

IF YOU CAN'T FIND ROUND MOLDS, USE FLAT, CIRCULAR ONES. YOUR LOLLIPOPS WILL HAVE A QUAINT, OLD-FASHIONED LOOK.

TIP

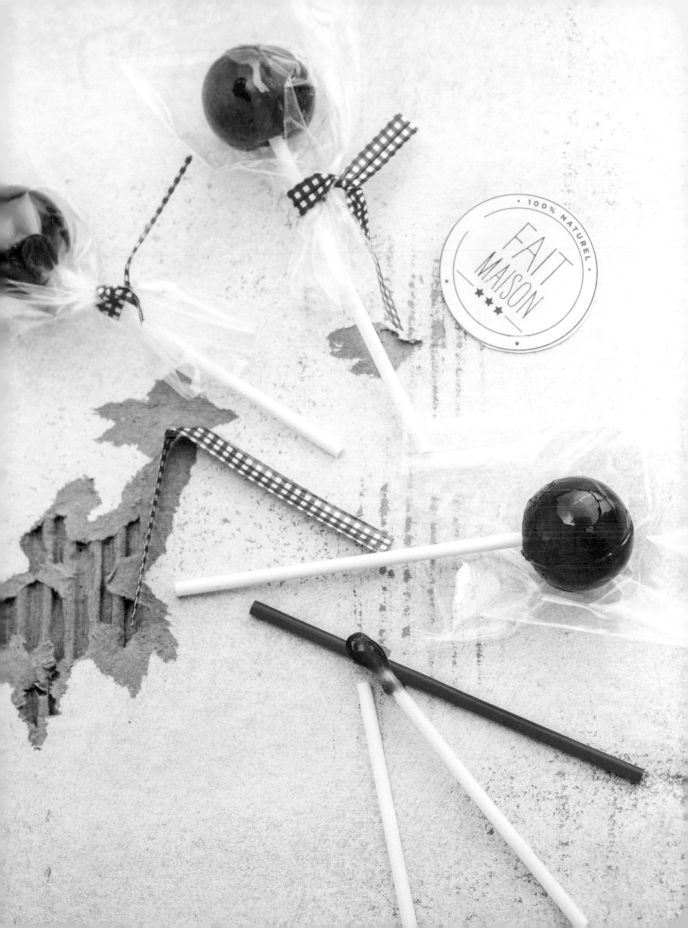

VENETIAN **ICE CREAM**

Vanilla ice cream and crispy chocolate: That's it! Bye-bye vegetable fat, glucose-fructose syrup, emulsifiers, stabilizers...

MAKES:
6 TO 8 SERVINGS

PREPARATION
about 20 minutes

COOKING
5 to 7 minutes

REFRIGERATION
30 minutes

FREEZING
6 hours

INGREDIENTS
Vanilla Ice Cream
(see page 127)

2 ounces bittersweet or
semisweet chocolate

| Make vanilla ice cream and when it is churning in the ice cream machine, cut the chocolate into pieces and melt in the top of a double boiler. Cover 2 baking sheets with parchment paper and pour the melted chocolate onto them, spreading it paper thin over the entire area with a rubber spatula. Refrigerate for 30 minutes to give the chocolate time to harden.

| When the chocolate has set, spread the vanilla ice cream thinly over the bottom of a 10-inch (25-cm) round springform pan. Cover with pieces of the chocolate broken off the sheets. Cover with another layer of ice cream, another layer of chocolate, and so on until you've used all the ice cream and chocolate.

| Smooth the surface, cover the pan with plastic wrap, and freeze for at least 6 hours.

| Remove the pan from the freezer 10 minutes before serving, dip the pan in hot water, turn out, and cut into slices. The ice cream will keep in the freezer for up to 1 month.

TIP

WHY NOT SPRINKLE SHARDS
OF CARAMEL ALONG WITH
THE CHOCOLATE OVER THE
ICE CREAM?

MYSTÈRES

The "mystery" of this ice cream dessert is that the vanilla ice cream is hidden inside a praline coating—homemade, of course.

MAKES:
6 SERVINGS

PREPARATION
about 40 minutes or the day before

FREEZING
2 hours

COOKING
55 to 65 minutes

STANDING TIME
30 minutes

MERINGUE

1 large egg white, preferably free-range

2 drops lemon juice

2 tablespoons granulated sugar

¼ cup (30 grams) confectioners' sugar

Vanilla Ice Cream (see page 127)

PRALINE

5 ounces (150 grams) whole hazelnuts in their skins

½ cup 2 tablespoons (150 grams) sugar

CARAMEL

½ cup (100 grams) granulated sugar

1 teaspoon honey

½ teaspoon lemon juice

MERINGUE

| Preheat the oven to 200°F (93°C).

| Whisk the egg white with the lemon juice until stiff, using an electric mixer. Continue whisking as you add the granulated sugar. When the egg white is shiny, add the confectioners' sugar and whisk for a few more seconds.

| Using a teaspoon or a pastry bag, cover a baking sheet lined with parchment paper with little blobs of meringue. Bake for 40 to 50 minutes until the egg white has hardened. Let the meringue cool before lifting off the paper.

| Use a silicone mold with hollows in the shape of hemispheres about 3 inches (7 cm) in diameter. Press the ice cream into the hollows until they're three-quarters full.

| Press a meringue into each cup holding ice cream until it envelopes the meringue. If necessary, add a little more ice cream so that the surface is completely smooth. Freeze the mold for 2 hours.

PRALINE

| Preheat the oven to 300°F (150°C).

| Spread the hazelnuts on a baking sheet and roast for about 15 minutes, until they're golden brown.

| Meanwhile, make the caramel, as described on page 24, using the sugar, honey, and lemon juice listed above. Add the roasted hazelnuts and mix to coat.

| Line a baking sheet with a silicone mat and pour the caramel on it. Spread it out and let it set at room temperature for 30 minutes. Break the caramel into pieces with your hands.

| Put the pieces of caramel in a blender and pulse into smaller pieces. Work in bursts and don't mix too long, or you'll wind up with ground hazelnuts.

| About 10 minutes before serving, transfer the ice cream, still in the molds, to the refrigerator to let it soften. Spread the broken praline on a plate, pry the ice cream from the mold, and roll the ice cream in the praline to coat. Serve right away, using any leftover meringue for decoration.

| The ice cream will keep for up to 1 month in the freezer.

SUPER-CREAMY
VANILLA ICE CREAM

Soft...creamy...melt-in-the-mouth...(sigh!)...truly sin on a spoon!

**MAKES:
ABOUT 1 QUART
(1 LITER)**

PREPARATION
about 15 minutes

STANDING TIME
15 minutes

COOKING
5 to 7 minutes

REFRIGERATION
2 hours

INGREDIENTS

1½ cups plus
2 tablespoons (40 cl)
skim milk

1⅔ cups (365 grams)
sour cream (30% fat)

¾ cup (170 grams)
sugar

Seeds of 1 vanilla bean

5 large egg yolks,
preferably free-range

| In a saucepan, stir together the milk, sour cream, and sugar.

| Split the vanilla bean in half lengthwise and scrape out the seeds. Add the seeds to the saucepan and bring to a boil. Remove from the heat, cover, and let sit for 15 minutes to give the vanilla time to permeate.

| Put the egg yolks in a bowl, gradually pour the milk mixture over the yolks, and stir well. Pour the mixture back into the saucepan and warm it over low heat for a few minutes, stirring continuously until it thickens into a custard – or, as the French call it, "English cream."

| Pour the custard into a bowl and cover with plastic wrap. Let the custard cool at room temperature before refrigerating for 2 hours.

| Transfer to an ice cream machine and make the ice cream following the manufacturer's instructions. Either serve immediately or freeze until required.

| The ice cream keeps for up to 1 month in the freezer (if it lasts that long!).

MULTICOLORED **ICE POPS**

A recipe so simple, kids can make their own ice pops.

MAKES:
8 ICE POPS

PREPARATION
about 10 minutes
(preferably the day
before)

FREEZING
3 hours

INGREDIENTS
1 part fruit juice or
nectar (your choice of
flavor)

4 parts water

| Mix the juice and water by measuring them with the molds you plan to use to form the pops. Use the actual molds to measure the juice and water. Pour the mixture into each of 8 popsicle molds. Freeze for 3 hours.

| If you can't find ice pop molds, use small plastic jars or empty yogurt containers. In this case, freeze the mixture for only 1 hour, then insert the popsicle sticks in the center and freeze for about 2 hours.

| For multicolored ice pops, make appropriate quantities of each mixture and pour 1 color into the bottom of each mold. Freeze for 1 hour and 30 minutes. Pour in the next color and freeze for 1 hour and 30 minutes. Repeat to make as many layers as you want. The popsicles will keep for up to 1 month in the freezer.

TIP

INSTEAD OF FRUIT
JUICE OR NECTAR, USE
FRUIT-FLAVORED SYRUPS.
BECAUSE THE SYRUPS HAVE
A HIGHER SUGAR CONTENT
THAN JUICE OR NECTAR,
THE RATIO OF SYRUP TO
WATER SHOULD BE 7:1.

NOTE

THE MIXTURE SHOULD BE 4 PARTS
WATER AND 1 PART JUICE OR NECTAR.
THE SIMPLEST WAY TO MEASURE IT
IS TO USE THE ICE POP MOLDS
THEMSELVES. WHATEVER SHAPE AND
SIZE THEY ARE, YOU'LL HAVE
THE RIGHT AMOUNT.

CHOCOLATE-COATED ICE CREAM POPS

MAKES:
6 LARGE ICE CREAM POPS

PREPARATION
about 30 minutes

STANDING TIME
15 minutes

COOKING
2 hours

REFRIGERATION
2 hours

FREEZING
2 hours

INGREDIENTS
Vanilla Ice Cream
(see page 127)

7 ounces (200 grams)
bittersweet, semisweet,
milk or while chocolate,
coarsely chopped

2 teaspoons oil, such
as sunflower, walnut,
hazelnut, or pistachio

¼ cup (50 grams)
chopped hazelnuts,
pistachios, or M&Ms

Once you've tasted the homemade version, you'll never want to buy them again.

| When you remove the ice cream from the ice cream maker, pour it into 6 ice pop molds, compressing it firmly, and freeze for 2 hours

| Remove the ice cream pops from the molds. Run them under hot water if necessary. Set the ice cream pops on a baking sheet lined with parchment paper. Return to the freezer.

| Melt the chocolate in the top of a double boiler. Try not to let it get hotter than 95°F (35°C), as shown on a candy thermometer. The melted chocolate will be as shiny as possible. Remove from the heat and stir in the oil.

| Dip the ice cream pops into the chocolate mixture, let the excess run off, and decorate with the chopped nuts or M&Ms. Freeze until required.

| The pops will keep for up to 1 month in the freezer.

ICE CREAM **SUNDAES**

A perfect end to a summer meal.

MAKES:
6 SERVINGS

PREPARATION
about 20 minutes

COOKING
about 15 minutes

FREEZING
30 minutes

ICE CREAM

5 large egg yolks,
preferably free-range

1½ cups plus
2 tablespoons (40 cl) skim
milk

1½ cups plus 2
tablespoons (40 cl)
heavy cream

¾ cup (170 grams) sugar

1 vanilla bean

PEANUTS

1 tablespoon sugar

4 ounces (125 grams)
unsalted peanuts (about
½ cup)

CARAMEL SAUCE

½ cup (125 grams) sugar

4 tablespoons (60 grams)
salted butter

3 tablespoons
mascarpone

CHOCOLATE SAUCE

4 ounces (125 grams)
bittersweet or semisweet
chocolate, coarsely
chopped

10 tablespoons (15 cl)
light cream

Other possibilities:
chocolate chips, pieces
of a crunchy chocolate
bar (see page 115), or
caramel candy (see
page 116)

| Make vanilla ice cream as described on page 127 using the ingredients listed here.

| Put 6 freezer-safe glass or earthenware dishes in the freezer.

| While the ice cream is setting, make the chosen topping(s):

PEANUTS

| Heat the oven to 325°F (170°C).

| Make a syrup by boiling the sugar in 1 tablespoon of water. Mix in the peanuts and then spread them over a baking sheet. Roast, stirring from time to time, until they darken in color and are aromatic. Be sure the peanuts don't burn.

CARAMEL SAUCE

| Caramelize the sugar in a pan, as described on page 24. Remove from the heat and vigorously mix in the butter, taking care not to splash yourself with hot sugar. Add the mascarpone and mix vigorously again.

CHOCOLATE SAUCE

| Melt the chocolate in the top of a double boiler. Remove from the heat, add the cream and mix well.

| When ready to serve, remove the dishes from the freezer, squirt the ice cream into them, using a pastry bag with a serrated nozzle, and top with the chosen topping and/or any of the other possibilities listed. Eat right away.

NOTE

PUTTING THE DISHES IN
THE FREEZER MEANS THAT THE
ICE CREAM WILL NOT MELT
QUICKLY. THIS GIVES YOU
MORE TIME TO ENJOY
THE SUNDAE.

GRENADINE SYRUP

MAKES:
1 16-OUNCE (50-CL)
BOTTLE

PREPARATION
about 25 minutes

COOKING
about 5 minutes

INGREDIENTS
3 large ripe
pomegranates

Granulated sugar (for
quantity, see recipe)

Juice of ¼ lemon

Most store-bought grenadine syrup is actually made from a variety of fruits (if you're lucky), but let's not forget that the real thing is made from pomegranates. Prepare to rediscover the original taste.

| Peel the pomegranates, remove the seeds, and squeeze the juice from the seeds. The simplest way to do this is to use a centrifuge. If you don't have one, put the seeds in a blender, and then filter the juice twice to make sure the juice is completely clear, with no bits of pith.

| Weigh the juice and mix with the same weight of sugar in a saucepan. Bring to a boil, then simmer over low heat for 10 minutes. Remove from the heat and mix in the lemon juice.

| Pour while still hot into a sterilized glass bottle (see page 140) and seal.

| To make grenadine juice, dilute 1 measure of syrup in 5 measures of water. The syrup will keep in a sealed bottle for up to 6 months.

NOTE

TO SEPARATE THE POMEGRANATE SEEDS FROM THE BITTER PITH, SUBMERGE THE PEELED FRUIT IN A LARGE BOWL OF WATER. THE PITH WILL FLOAT TO THE SURFACE AND THE SEEDS WILL SINK TO THE BOTTOM.

MINT SYRUP

This 100% natural syrup might not be bright green, like the mint syrup you can buy (no food coloring allowed here), but it tastes incredible.

MAKES:
1¼ CUPS (30 CL)

PREPARATION
about 10 minutes

STANDING TIME
6 to 8 hours

COOKING
about 10 minutes

INGREDIENTS
1 ounce (30 grams)
fresh mint (2 large
bunches)

½ cup plus
2 tablespoons
(150 grams) sugar

2 teaspoons lemon juice

| Pull the leaves off the stalks of mint. Rinse and dry in a salad spinner.

| Bring 1¼ cups (30 cl) of water to a boil. Pour it over the leaves, cover, and let sit for 6 to 8 hours or until the water is fully flavored.

| Pour the syrup through a filter or fine-mesh sieve. Squeeze the leaves to extract every last drop of flavor.

| Add the sugar and lemon juice, bring to a boil, and simmer for about 10 minutes over a low heat, stirring until the sugar melts.

| Pour into a sterilized container (see page 140) while still hot and seal. The syrup will keep for 2 to 3 months if unopened and for 1 month in the refrigerator if opened.

NOTE

TO GIVE THE SYRUP AN
EVEN MINTIER FLAVOR, ADD
3 STALKS OF WILD MINT TO
THE INFUSION—ENOUGH
TO MAKE YOUR HAIR
STAND ON END.

ICED TEA

MAKES:
1 QUART (1 LITER)

PREPARATION
about 10 minutes

REFRIGERATION
overnight plus 1 hour

INGREDIENTS
⅓ cup (80 ml) sugar syrup

2 pinches baking soda

2 teaspoons loose tea leaves

1 small piece cinnamon stick

PEACH FLAVORING

2 white peaches

2 teaspoons lemon juice

CITRUS FLAVORING

1 orange, preferably organic

1 lemon, preferably organic

In the days before canned tea, iced tea was served in a pretty glass pitcher after infusing overnight. Revive the tradition with this simple recipe.

| Dissolve the sugar syrup and baking soda in about 1 quart (1 liter) of cold water.

| Fill a tea infuser ball with the loose tea (your favorite kind) and drop it into the water with the cinnamon. Refrigerate overnight.

| The next morning, remove the tea infuser and add your chosen flavoring.

PEACH FLAVORING

| Peel and pit the peaches. Put them in a blender and process to a puree. Add the lemon juice and the puree to the tea. Strain and refrigerate the flavored tea until ready to serve.

CITRUS FLAVORING

| Grate the zest of ½ of the orange and lemon and add to the tea. Squeeze both the orange and lemon and stir the juice into the tea. Refrigerate for at least 1 hour and then serve.

| The iced tea will keep in the refrigerator for up to 3 days.

THE BAKING SODA PREVENTS THE TEA FROM BECOMING BITTER, WHICH IT MIGHT OTHERWISE DO IF LEFT TO INFUSE FOR SEVERAL HOURS.

NOTE

137

TRADITIONAL **LEMONADE**

**MAKES:
1 QUART (1 LITER)**

PREPARATION
about 10 minutes

STANDING TIME
4 to 5 days

INGREDIENTS
1 lemon, preferably
organic

½ cup (100 grams)
sugar

1 teaspoon cider
vinegar

It's possible to make lemonade with carbonated water or soda, but the traditional French method is to let a lemon solution ferment.

| Cut the lemon, including skin, into small pieces. Remove the seeds.

| Boil 1 quart (1 liter) of water in a large saucepan and stir in the sugar, vinegar, and lemon pieces.

| Cover and leave to ferment for 4 to 5 days at room temperature. The lemonade should start to fizz slightly.

| Filter or strain the lemonade and pour it into a sterilized glass bottle (see page 140). Leave about 2 inches (5 cm) of room at the top of the bottle. Refrigerate. The lemonade will keep for up to 10 days in the refrigerator.

QUICK **FIZZY LEMONADE**

**MAKES:
1 QUART (1 LITER)**

PREPARATION
about 5 minutes

REFRIGERATION:
2 hours

INGREDIENTS
2 large lemons,
preferably organic

2 teaspoons sugar syrup
or agave syrup

3 cups (70 cl)
carbonated water

| Wash the lemons thoroughly in hot water. Cut the lemons, including the skins, into small pieces. Remove the seeds.

| Put the lemon in a blender with 7 tablespoons (10 cl) of water and the sugar syrup and blend to a thick paste.

| Mix the paste with the carbonated water and refrigerate for 2 hours. Filter or strain just before serving. The lemonade will keep for up to 1 week in the refrigerator.

A FEW USEFUL **TRICKS OF THE TRADE**

STERILIZING CONTAINERS

If you want to keep jams, spreads, ketchup, or drinks, you should always use sterilized containers. There are two ways of sterilizing things (in both cases, you should wash them thoroughly first):

| Soak the containers for 15 minutes in boiling water (don't forget the lids!).

| Heat the oven to 300°F (150°C) and leave the containers inside for 20 minutes.

| Don't fill the sterilized container right to the top but leave a little head room. Screw on the lid so that it's a tight fit, then turn the jars upside down so that the jar's hot contents sterilize the lid and there is no longer any air between the lid and the contents. When cool, turn the jars upright for storing. That way, they'll keep even longer.

TEMPERING CHOCOLATE

Unfortunately, there's no simple magic formula for making chocolate coatings glossy and crunchy. The chocolate must be "tempered," which means heating and cooling the chocolate to specific temperatures, then gently reheating it (it's all got to do with the crystallization of the cocoa butter content), and for this you'll need a candy thermometer. If all this sounds too complicated, don't worry: Your cakes and biscuits will taste just as good, although they'll look rather dull. But if you want to wow your guests like a pro, here's what to do:

| Bittersweet and semisweet chocolate: Melt and heat to around 120°F (49°C). Let the chocolate cool to 80°F (27°C) before reheating to 86° to 90°F (30° to 32°C).

| Milk chocolate: Melt and heat to 113°F (45°C), let cool to 81°F (27°C), and reheat no higher than 86°F (30°C).

| A simple method is to use your freezer. Creating a "thermal shock" between the mixture to be coated and the melted chocolate helps to form a smooth, shiny coating. Just put whatever you want to coat (cookies, bars, etc.) in the freezer for 15 to 30 minutes. Dip the cookie, bar, etc., in the melted chocolate one by one, straight from the freezer. This will make the chocolate crystallize and harden in seconds, creating a smoother coating, with a more satisfying "crunch."

ROLLING PASTRY AND DOUGH THINLY

The dough for cookies and other baked goods is often sticky stuff and not easy to roll out. It's therefore essential to refrigerate it. It's best to wrap it in plastic wrap and refrigerate it before rolling it out for cutting into shapes.

The simplest way of avoiding using too much flour for rolling, which alters both the taste and the texture of the dough, is to roll it between two silicone mats or sheets of parchment paper.

CUTTING OUT PASTRY SHAPES

Very thin pastry easily tears. To avoid tearing, use a pastry or cookie cutter rather than a knife. Even better is a sharp pizza wheel: It's quicker, too.

FREQUENTLY ASKED QUESTIONS

WHAT I'VE MADE IS GOOD, BUT IT'S NOT QUITE THE SAME AS THE EQUIVALENT SUPERMARKET PRODUCT. WHY?

Most of the recipes in this book are based on supermarket products and use essentially the same ingredients. We've found substitutes for the ones that are really hard to find, as well as the controversial ones, such as glucose-fructose syrup, palm oil, and anything that adds nothing to the taste (colorings, emulsifiers, etc.).

Glucose-fructose syrup, for example, has been replaced by ordinary sugar, sometimes supplemented with honey, which adds moisture and therefore softens the mixture—especially when baking cakes.

As for fats, product labels often mention "vegetable fats" or "vegetable oils." These include solid, hydrogenated vegetable oils, which are both unhealthy and harmful to the environment. We think you're better off without them. So, depending on the recipe, we've replaced them with canola or sunflower oil, butter, or a combination of the two.

Finally, since nothing you're making needs to be kept for months on end, we've steered clear of emulsifiers and preservatives. More good news!

WHY CAN'T MY HOMEMADE PRODUCTS BE KEPT FOR AS LONG AS THE ONES I BUY?

First, your kitchen is not a sterile food factory. What's more, as we've said, our recipes contain no preservatives. Nevertheless, there are a few ways to make your homemade goodies last just a bit longer:

Add a few drops of white vinegar or lemon juice to any dough (buns, bread, etc.).

When buying ingredients that won't be cooked (for example, for muesli), choose the ones with the latest sell-by dates. This means your product will keep longer.

For dairy products (yogurt, custard, etc.), use sterilized containers.

INDEX